# Kindergarten

## Teacher's Edition

Welcome to Kindergarten

**Senior Authors** J. David Cooper, John J. Pikulski
**Authors** Patricia A. Ackerman, Kathryn H. Au, David J. Chard, Gilbert G. Garcia, Claude N. Goldenberg, Marjorie Y. Lipson, Susan E. Page, Shane Templeton, Sheila W. Valencia, MaryEllen Vogt

**Consultants** Linda H. Butler, Linnea C. Ehri, Carla B. Ford

 HOUGHTON MIFFLIN    BOSTON • MORRIS PLAINS, NJ

California • Colorado • Georgia • Illinois • New Jersey • Texas

## Literature Reviewers

*Consultants:* **Dr. Adela Artola Allen**, Associate Dean, Graduate College, Associate Vice President for Inter-American Relations, University of Arizona, Tucson, Arizona; **Dr. Manley Begay**, Co-director of the Harvard Project on American Indian Economic Development, Director of the National Executive Education Program for Native Americans, Harvard University, John F. Kennedy School of Government, Cambridge, Massachusetts; **Dr. Nicholas Kannellos**, Director, Arte Publico Press, Director, Recovering the U.S. Hispanic Literacy Heritage Project, University of Houston, Texas; **Mildred Lee**, author and former head of Library Services for Sonoma County, Santa Rosa, California; **Dr. Barbara Moy**, Director of the Office of Communication Arts, Detroit Public Schools, Michigan; **Norma Naranjo**, Clark County School District, Las Vegas, Nevada; **Dr. Arlette Ingram Willis**, Associate Professor, Department of Curriculum and Instruction, Division of Language and Literacy, University of Illinois at Urbana-Champaign, Illinois

*Teachers:* **Helen Brooks**, Vestavia Hills Elementary School, Birmingham, Alabama; **Patricia Buchanan**, Thurgood Marshall School, Newark, Delaware; **Gail Connor**, Language Arts Resource Teacher, Duval County, Jacksonville, Florida; **Vicki DeMott**, McClean Science/Technology School, Wichita, Kansas; **Marge Egenhoffer**, Dixon Elementary School, Brookline, Wisconsin; **Mary Jew Mori**, Griffin Avenue Elementary, Los Angeles, California

## Program Reviewers

*Supervisors:* **Judy Artz**, Middletown Monroe City School District, Ohio; **James Bennett**, Elkhart Schools, Elkhart, Indiana; **Kay Buckner-Seal**, Wayne County, Michigan; **Charlotte Carr**, Seattle School District, Washington; **Sister Marion Christi**, St. Matthews School, Archdiocese of Philadelphia, Pennsylvania; **Alvina Crouse**, Garden Place Elementary, Denver Public Schools, Colorado; **Peggy DeLapp**, Minneapolis, Minnesota; **Carol Erlandson**, Wayne Township Schools, Marion County, Indianapolis; **Brenda Feeney**, North Kansas City School District, Missouri; **Winnie Huebsch**, Sheboygan Area Schools, Wisconsin; **Brenda Mickey**, Winston-Salem/Forsyth County Schools, North Carolina; **Audrey Miller**, Sharpe Elementary School, Camden, New Jersey; **JoAnne Piccolo**, Rocky Mountain Elementary, Adams 12 District, Colorado; **Sarah Rentz**, East Baton Rouge Parish School District, Louisiana; **Kathy Sullivan**, Omaha Public Schools, Nebraska; **Rosie Washington**, Kuny Elementary, Gary, Indiana; **Theresa Wishart**, Knox County Public Schools, Tennessee

*Teachers:* **Carol Brockhouse**, Madison Schools, Wayne Westland Schools, Michigan; **Eva Jean Conway**, R.C. Hill School, Valley View School District, Illinois; **Carol Daley**, Jane Addams School, Sioux Falls, South Dakota; **Karen Landers**, Watwood Elementary, Talladega County, Alabama; **Barb LeFerrier**, Mullenix Ridge Elementary, South Kitsap District, Port Orchard, Washington; **Loretta Piggee**, Nobel School, Gary, Indiana; **Cheryl Remash**, Webster Elementary School, Manchester, New Hampshire; **Marilynn Rose**, Michigan; **Kathy Scholtz**, Amesbury Elementary School, Amesbury, Massachusetts; **Dottie Thompson**, Erwin Elementary, Jefferson County, Alabama; **Dana Vassar**, Moore Elementary School, Winston-Salem, North Carolina; **Joy Walls**, Ibraham Elementary School, Winston-Salem, North Carolina; **Elaine Warwick**, Fairview Elementary, Williamson County, Tennessee

## Credits

*Cover*
(tl) Eyewire, (tr) FPG Royalty Free, (b) Comstock KLIPS

*Theme Opener*
(t) FPG Royalty Free, (m) Eyewire, (b) The Stock Market Royalty Free

*Assignment Photography*
Parker/Boon Productions
pp. T27, T33

Joel Benjamin
pp. T21, T43, T75, T99, T123, T131, T149

## Acknowledgments

Grateful acknowledgment is made for permission to reprint copyrighted material as follows:

*Theme 7*
*Mr. Gumpy's Motor Car,* by John Burningham. Copyright © 1973 by John Burningham. Reprinted by permission of HarperCollins Publishers.

*The Little Engine That Could,* retold by Watty Piper, illustrated by George and Doris Hauman. Copyright © 1976, 1961, 1954, 1945, 1930 by Platt & Munk Publishers, a division of Grosset & Dunlap Inc., which is a division of Penguin Putnam Inc. Reprinted by permission of Grosset & Dunlap Inc., a division of Penguin Putnam Inc.

*The Wheels on the Bus,* by Maryann Kovalski. Copyright © 1987 by Maryann Kovalski. Reprinted by arrangement with Kids Can Press Ltd. (Toronto, Canada) and Little, Brown and Company (New York).

*Vroom, Chugga, Vroom-Vroom,* by Anne Miranda, illustrated by David Murphy. Text copyright © 1998 by Anne Miranda. Illustrations copyright © 1998 by David Murphy. Reprinted by permission of Turtle Books.

Lodge
Textbook
PE
1119
.H68
2001
Gr. K
TE
Th. 7

**3 wheels**

**4 wheels**

**6 wheels**

# Wheels Go Around

### OBJECTIVES

**Phonemic Awareness** blending phonemes

**Phonics** sounds for letters *D, d; Z, z*

**Decoding** *-ig* word family

**High-Frequency Words** recognize two new high-frequency words

**Reading Strategies** summarize; monitor/clarify; question; phonics/decoding

**Comprehension Skills** text organization and summarizing; cause and effect; making predictions

**Vocabulary** opposites; position words; parts of a car; words for travel

**Writing** signs; journals; class story; report

**Listening/Speaking/Viewing** activities to support vocabulary expansion and writing

# Wheels Go Around
## *Literature Resources*

## WEEK 1

### Teacher Read Aloud
**Wheels Around**
*nonfiction by Shelley Rotner*
pages T10–T11

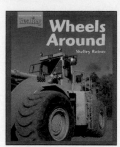

### Big Book
**The Wheels on the Bus**
*fiction by Maryann Kovalski*
pages T18–T19, T28–T33

### Science Link
**Look for Wheels**
*nonfiction*
pages T40–T41

### Decodable Phonics Library
**Big Rig**
page T35

Big Rig
by Amy Griffin
illustrated by Bob Kolar

## WEEK 2

### Teacher Read Aloud
**The Little Engine That Could**
*fiction retold by Watty Piper*
pages T62–T65

### Big Book
**Vroom, Chugga, Vroom-Vroom**
*fantasy by Anne Miranda*
pages T72–T73, T82–T89

### Science Link
**Cool Wheels!**
*nonfiction*
pages T96–T97

### Decodable Phonics Library
**Tan Van**
page T91

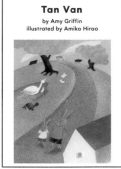

Tan Van
by Amy Griffin
illustrated by Amiko Hirao

## WEEK 3

### Teacher Read Aloud
**Mr. Gumpy's Motor Car**
*a contemporary British tale by John Burningham*
pages T118–T121

### Revisit the Big Books:
**The Wheels on the Bus**
pages T128–T129

**Vroom, Chugga, Vroom-Vroom**
pages T138–T139

### Revisit the Links:
### Science
**Look for Wheels**
page T146

### Science
**Cool Wheels!**
page T147

### Decodable Phonics Library
**Zig Pig and Dan Cat**
page T141

Zig Pig and Dan Cat
by Amy Griffin
illustrated by Amiko Hirao

# Big Books for Use All Year

From Apples
to Zebras:
A Book of ABC's

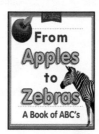

Higglety Pigglety:
A Book of Rhymes

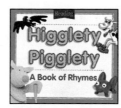

# Leveled Books

See Cumulative Listing of Leveled Books.

## Phonics Library

**Decodable**

- Big Rig
- Tan Van
- Zig Pig and
  Dan Cat

Lessons, pages
T35, T91, T141

## On My Way Practice Reader

**Easy** / **On Level**

### Dig, Zig Pig!
*by Sam Fonte*
page T155

## Little Big Books

**On Level** / **Challenge**

The Wheels
on the Bus

Vroom, Chugga,
Vroom-Vroom

## 🎞 Audiotape

Wheels Go Around

## Houghton Mifflin
## Classroom Bookshelf

Level K

## Little Readers
## for Guided Reading

Collection K

# Bibliography

## Books for Browsing

### ABCDrive!*
by Naomi Howland
Clarion 2000 (32p)
A boy on a car trip sees things related to vehicles for every letter of the alphabet.

### This Train
by Paul Collicut
Farrar 1999 (32p)
Pictures of trains and brief sentences in large type demonstrate opposites and simple contrasts.

###  Beep Beep, Vroom Vroom!
by Stuart J. Murphy
Harper 2000 (40p) paper
Molly plays with her brother's toy cars, but can she put them back in the right order before her brother comes home?

###  So Many Circles, So Many Squares
by Tana Hoban
Greenwillow 1998 (32p)

The geometric concepts of circles and squares are presented in photos of wheels, signs, and other objects.

###  Delivery
by Anastasia Suen
Viking 1999 (32p)
Trucks, bicycles, taxis, and other vehicles deliver everything from newspapers to groceries.

###  Circular Movement
by Lola M. Schaefer
Pebble 2000 (24p)

Photographs and simple text describe objects that move in circles.

## Traffic Jam
by Seymour Chwast
Houghton 1999 (32p)
In a book with fold-out pages, a cat and her kitten cause a traffic jam when they cross the road.

###  Night at the Fair
by Donald Crews
Greenwillow 1998 (32p)
Nighttime is a great time to be at the fair, and the best ride of all is the giant Ferris wheel.

### Cars
by Gail Saunders-Smith
Pebble 1998 (24p)
Photographs and word pairs describe different kinds of cars.

### My Puffer Train
by Mary Murphy
Houghton 1999 (32p)
On the way to the seashore in his train, Penguin invites other animals aboard.

### Bear on a Bike
by Stella Blackstone
Barefoot 1999 (32p)
A bear tries out various modes of transportation.

## Books for Teacher Read Aloud

###  Mike Mulligan and His Steam Shovel
by Virginia Lee Burton
Houghton 1939 (48p) also paper
Mike and his steam shovel, Mary Anne, don't give up when they lose their job. **Available in Spanish as Mike Mulligan y su maquina maravillosa.**

### Curious George Rides a Bike
by H. A. Rey
Houghton 1952 (48p)
Curious George helps a boy with his paper route and gets into all sorts of trouble.

###  Fire Engines
by Marcia S. Freeman
Pebble 1999 (24p)
A simple description of fire engines and the equipment they carry.

### Duck in the Truck
by Jez Alborough
Harper 2000 (32p)
A frog, a goat, and a sheep help Duck when his truck gets stuck.

### On the Move
by Henry Pluckrose
Watts 1998 (32p) also paper
Photos and text present all kinds of vehicles that help people get from place to place.

### Truck Talk
by Bobbi Katz
Cartwheel 1997 (32p)
In poems paired with photos, trucks talk about what they do.

### Window Music
by Anastasia Suen
Viking 1998 (32p)
A train clickety clacks its way over hills and through valleys.

### The Little Engine That Could
by Watty Piper
Putnam 1930 (48p) also paper
A small but determined train engine helps get food and toys to children waiting in a valley.
**Available in Spanish as La pequeña locomotora que sí pudo.**

### Key

- 🔬 Science
- 🌐 Social Studies
- 🌍 Multicultural
- 🎸 Music
- 🔲 Math
- ⭐ Classic
- 🎨 Art

* = Included in Houghton Mifflin Classroom Bookshelf, Level K

**How Do You Lift a Lion?**
by Robert E. Wells
Whitman 1996 (32p) also paper
A simple look at how levers, pulleys, and wheels help to move heavy objects.

 **Seymour Simon's Book of Trucks**
by Seymour Simon
Harper 2000 (32p)
Photographs of trucks accompany descriptions of the jobs they do.

## Books for Shared Reading

 **Seals on the Bus**
by Lenny Hort
Holt 2000 (32p)
At every stop, animals join a family riding a bus in this popular song.

**Sheep in a Jeep***
by Nancy Shaw
Houghton 1986 (32p)
Five sheep out for a ride in their Jeep run into trouble.

 **Down By the Station**
by Will Hillenbrand
Harcourt 1999 (32p)
In this version of a familiar song, baby animals ride to the children's zoo on a train.

**Beep! Beep!**
by Anne Miranda
Turtle 1999 (32p)
A boy imagines himself to be many different vehicles, from a jeep to a rocket.

**Five Little Monkeys Wash the Car**
by Eileen Christelow
Clarion 2000 (32p)
Five monkeys try to persuade their crocodile neighbors to buy their old car. See others in series.

**The Train Ride**
by June Crebbin
Candlewick 1995 (32p) also paper
In a story with patterned text, a girl traveling by train to her grand-mother's watches the world go by her window.

## Books for Phonics Read Aloud

**Dazzling Diggers**
by Tony Mitton
Kingfisher 1997 (24p)
Animals operate digging machines that move rubble and do other things in this rhyming story.

**Mama Zooms**
by Jane Cowen-Fletcher
Scholastic 1993 (32p) also paper
A boy pretends his mama's wheelchair is everything from a racehorse to a spaceship.

**Zeely Zebra**
by Barbara Derubertis
Kane 1997 (32p) also paper
Zeely Zebra dreams of making the All-Star Racing team.

* = Included in Houghton Mifflin Classroom Bookshelf, Level K

## Technology

### Computer Software Resources

- **Curious George® Learns Phonics**
- **Lexia Quick Reading Test**
- **Lexia Phonics Based Reading**
- **Published by Sunburst Technology ***
  *Tenth Planet™ Vowels: Short and Long*
  *Curious George® Pre-K ABCs*
  *First Phonics*
- **Published by The Learning Company**
  *Dr. Seuss's ABC™*
  *Paint, Write, & Play!™*
  *¡Vamos a Jugar, Pintar, y Escribir!*

### Video Cassettes

- **The Alphabet Train.** *Big Kids*
- **Mike Mulligan and His Steam Shovel** *by Virginia Lee Burton. Weston Woods*
- **Cars! Cars! Cars!** *Big Kids*
- **The Little Engine That Could** *by Watty Piper. Weston Woods*
- **I Dig Dirt.** *Big Kids*
- **Curious George Rides a Bike** *by H. A. Rey. Weston Woods*
- **Big Work Trucks.** *Big Kids*
- **Fire Trucks in Action.** *Big Kids*

### Audio Cassettes

- **Sheep in a Jeep** *by Margot Apple. Houghton*
- **Truck Song** *by Diane Siebert. Live Oak*
- **The Bear's Bicycle** *by Emilie Warren McLeod. Live Oak*
- **Choo Choo** *by Virginia Lee Burton. Houghton*
- **Audiotapes for *Wheels Go Around*.** *Houghton Mifflin Company*

* © Sunburst Technology Corporation, a Houghton Mifflin Company. All Rights Reserved.
Technology Resources addresses are on page R8.

**Education Place**
**www.eduplace.com** *Log on to Education Place for more activities relating to* Wheels Go Around.
**Book Adventure**
**www.bookadventure.org** *This Internet reading-incentive program provides thousands of titles for students to read.*

# Theme 7

# Theme at a Glance

**Theme Concept:** *Wheels help us work and play, sometimes in unexpected ways.*

✓ **Indicates Tested Skills**

## Learning to Read

| | Phonemic Awareness and Phonics | High-Frequency Words | Comprehension Skills and Strategies |
|---|---|---|---|
| **WEEK 1**<br><br>**Read Aloud**<br>**Wheels Around**<br><br>**Big Book**<br>**The Wheels on the Bus**<br><br>**Science Link**<br>**Look for Wheels**<br><br>**Phonics Library**<br>*"Big Rig"* | ✓ Phonemic Awareness: Blending Phonemes, *T9, T17, T27, T39, T47*<br><br>✓ Initial Consonant *d, T12–T13, T20–T21*<br><br>✓ Blending *-ig* words, *T34, T42–T43*<br><br>**Phonics Review:** Familiar Consonants; *-ig, -it, -an, -at* words, *T13, T20, T36, T44, T50, T52* | ✓ High-Frequency Words, *T22–T23, T35, T51*<br><br>**Word Wall,** *T8, T16, T26, T38, T46* | ✓ Comprehension: Text Organization and Summarizing, *T10, T18, T29, T30, T31, T40, T48*<br><br>**Strategies:** Summarize, *T10, T18, T29, T32, T40*<br><br>**Phonics/Decoding,** *T35* |
| **WEEK 2**<br><br>**Read Aloud**<br>**The Little Engine That Could**<br><br>**Big Book**<br>**Vroom, Chugga, Vroom-Vroom**<br><br>**Science Link**<br>**Cool Wheels!**<br><br>**Phonics Library**<br>*"Tan Van"* | ✓ Phonemic Awareness: Blending Phonemes, *T61, T71, T81, T95, T103*<br><br>✓ Initial Consonant *z, T66–T67, T74–T75*<br><br>✓ Blending *-ig* words, *T90, T98–T99*<br><br>**Phonics Review:** Familiar Consonants; *-ig, -it, -at, -an* words, *T67, T74, T92, T100, T106, T108* | ✓ High-Frequency Words, *T76–T77, T91, T107*<br><br>**Word Wall,** *T60, T70, T80, T94, T102* | ✓ Comprehension: Cause and Effect, *T62, T72, T83, T85, T87, T96, T104*<br><br>**Strategies:** Monitor/Clarify, *T62, T72, T83, T84, T86, T96*<br><br>**Phonics/Decoding,** *T91* |
| **WEEK 3**<br><br>**Read Aloud**<br>**Mr. Gumpy's Motor Car**<br><br>**Big Books**<br>**The Wheels on the Bus**<br>**Vroom, Chugga, Vroom-Vroom**<br><br>**Science Links**<br>**Look for Wheels**<br>**Cool Wheels!**<br><br>**Phonics Library**<br>*"Zig Pig and Dan Cat"* | ✓ Phonemic Awareness: Blending Phonemes, *T117, T127, T137, T145, T153*<br><br>✓ Review Initial Consonants *d, z, T122–T123, T130–T131*<br><br>✓ Blending *-ig* words, *T140, T148–T149*<br><br>**Phonics Review:** Familiar Consonants; *-ig, -it, -at, -an* words, *T123, T130, T142, T150, T156, T158* | High-Frequency Words, *T132–T133, T141, T157*<br><br>**Word Wall,** *T116, T126, T136, T144, T152* | ✓ Comprehension: Making Predictions, *T118, T128, T129, T138, T139, T146, T147, T154*<br><br>**Strategies:** Summarize, *T146*<br><br>**Question,** *T118, T128, T129, T138, T139*<br><br>**Phonics/Decoding,** *T141* |

Big Rig
by Amy Griffin
illustrated by Bob Kolar

Tan Van
by Amy Griffin
illustrated by Amika Hiroo

Zig Pig and Dan Cat
by Amy Griffin
illustrated by Amika Hiroo

## Pacing

- This theme is designed to take approximately 3 weeks, depending on your students' needs.

## Multi-age Classroom

**Related theme—**

- **Grade 1:** *We Can Do It!*

## Technology

**Education Place: www.eduplace.com** Log on to Education Place for more activities relating to *Wheels Go Around.*

**Lesson Planner CD-ROM:** Customize your planning for *Wheels Go Around* with the Lesson Planner.

| Word Work | | Writing & Language | | | Centers |
|---|---|---|---|---|---|
| **High-Frequency Word Practice** | **Building Words** | **Oral Language** | **Writing** | **Listening/ Speaking/Viewing** | **Content Area** |
| Matching Words, *T14*<br>Building Sentences, *T24* | Word Family *-ig*, *T36*<br>Word Families *-ig, -it, -an*, *T44*<br>Word Families, *T52* | **Using Opposites**<br>• opposites chart, *T15*<br>**Vocabulary Expansion**<br>• opposites chart, *T25* | **Shared Writing**<br>• writing about signs, *T37*<br>**Interactive Writing**<br>• writing about signs, *T45*<br>**Independent Writing**<br>• Journals, *T53* | Viewing and Speaking, *T25, T37*<br>Listening, Viewing, and Speaking, *T45* | Book Center, *T11*<br>Phonics Center, *T13, T21, T43*<br>Writing Center, *T15, T45*<br>Science Center, *T19*<br>Art Center, *T25*<br>Dramatic Play Center, *T33* |
| Matching Words, *T68*<br>Building Sentences, *T78* | Word Family *-ig*, *T92*<br>Word Families *-ig, -it, -at*, *T100*<br>Word Families *-at, -an, -it, -ig*, *T108* | **Using Position Words**<br>• words that tell where things are, *T69*<br>**Vocabulary Expansion**<br>• position words, parts of a car, *T79* | **Shared Writing**<br>• writing a class story, *T93*<br>**Interactive Writing**<br>• writing a class story, *T101*<br>**Independent Writing**<br>• Journals, *T109* | Viewing, *T69*<br>Viewing and Speaking, *T79*<br>Listening, *T93* | Book Center, *T63, T109*<br>Phonics Center, *T67, T75, T99*<br>Writing Center, *T69, T101*<br>Dramatic Play Center, *T63, T79*<br>Science Center, *T73*<br>Math Center, *T89*<br>Art Center, *T89* |
| Matching Words, *T124*<br>Building Sentences, *T134* | Word Family *-ig*, *T142*<br>Word Families *-ig, -it, -at*, *T150*<br>Word Families, *T158* | **Using Opposites**<br>• more opposites, *T125*<br>**Vocabulary Expansion**<br>• words for travel, *T135* | **Shared Writing**<br>• writing a report, *T143*<br>**Interactive Writing**<br>• writing a report, *T151*<br>**Independent Writing**<br>• Journals, *T159* | Listening and Speaking, *T125, T135*<br>Speaking and Viewing, *T143*<br>Viewing and Speaking, *T151* | Book Center, *T119, T139*<br>Phonics Center, *T123, T131, T149*<br>Writing Center, *T125, T129, T151*<br>Dramatic Play Center, *T119*<br>Art Center, *T135, T139, T147* |

# Planning for Assessment

Use these resources to meet your assessment needs. For additional information, see the *Teacher's Assessment Handbook.*

Emerging Literacy Survey

Lexia CD-ROM

## Diagnostic Planning

### Emerging Literacy Survey

- If you have used this survey to obtain baseline data on the skills children brought with them to kindergarten, this might be a good time to re-administer all or parts of the survey to chart progress, to identify areas of strength and need, and to test the need for early intervention.

### Lexia Quick Phonics Assessment CD-ROM

- Can be used to identify students who need more help with phonics.

## Ongoing Assessment

### Phonemic Awareness:
- **Practice Book,** pp. 195–196, 205–206, 215–216

### Phonics:
- **Practice Book,** pp. 197, 200–201, 207, 210–211, 217, 220–221

### Comprehension:
- **Practice Book** Reading Responses, pp. 193–194, 199, 203–204, 209, 213–214, 219

### Writing:
- Writing samples for portfolios

### Informal Assessment:
- **Diagnostic Checks,** pp. T23, T33, T43, T51, T77, T88, T99, T107, T133, T149, T157

Integrated Theme Test

Theme Skills Test

## End-of-Theme Assessment

### Integrated Theme Test:
- Assesses children's progress as readers and writers in a format that reflects instruction. Simple decodable texts test reading skills in context.

### Theme Skills Test:
- Assesses children's mastery of specific reading and language arts skills taught in the theme.

# Kindergarten Benchmarks

For your planning, listed here are the instructional goals and activities that help develop benchmark behaviors for kindergartners. Use this list to plan instruction and to monitor children's progress. See the Checklist of skills found on p. T161.

| Theme Lessons and Activities: | Benchmark Behaviors: |
| --- | --- |
| **Oral Language**<br>• rhymes, chants, motion songs<br>• shared reading | • can listen to story attentively<br>• can participate in the shared reading experience |
| **Phonemic Awareness**<br>• blending phonemes<br>• beginning sounds | • can blend sounds into meaningful units |
| **Phonics**<br>• initial consonants *d, z*<br>• word family *-ig* | • can name single letters and their sounds<br>• can decode some common CVC words |
| **Concepts of Print**<br>• first/last letter of a written word<br>• all capital letters for emphasis<br>• matching spoken words to print<br>• matching words | • can recognize common print conventions |
| **Reading**<br>• decodable texts<br>• high-frequency words *for, have* | • can read and write a few words<br>• can select a letter to represent a sound |
| **Comprehension**<br>• text organization and summarizing<br>• cause and effect<br>• inferences: making predictions | • can think critically about a text<br>• can use effective reading strategies |
| **Writing and Language**<br>• drawing and labeling images<br>• writing simple phrases or sentences<br>• using opposites and position words<br>• journal writing | • can label pictures using phonetic spellings<br>• can write independently |

# Launching the Theme
## *Wheels Go Around*

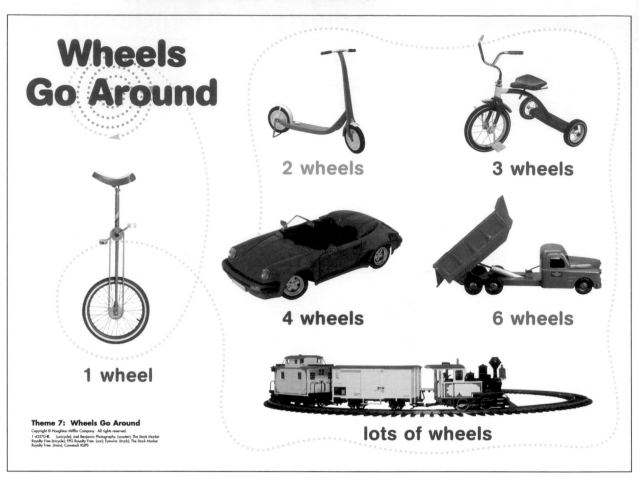

**Wheels Go Around**

1 wheel

2 wheels

3 wheels

4 wheels

6 wheels

lots of wheels

Theme 7: Wheels Go Around
Copyright © Houghton Mifflin Company. All rights reserved.
1-43570-K     (unicycle): Joel Benjamin Photography. (scooter): The Stock Market
Royalty Free. (tricycle); FPG Royalty Free. (car); Eyewire. (truck); The Stock Market
Royalty Free. (train); Comstock KLIPS

**Theme Poster: Wheels Go Around**

## ▶ Using the Theme Poster

In this theme, children will learn about all kinds of wheels. Display the Theme Poster, see how many of the vehicles children recognize, and compare the numbers and types of wheels. During the theme, children can tape on captioned drawings to extend Poster learnings.

- **Week 1** Two good sources of information are the Read Aloud *Wheels Around* and the Science Link *Look for Wheels.* After sharing these selections, children can add drawings or magazine pictures to the Poster to show unusual wheels such as a merry-go-round, a Ferris wheel, or a hamster's wheel.
- **Week 2** The Science Link *Cool Wheels!* features people-powered and motor-powered vehicles. Children can rearrange the drawings on their poster into those categories or others.
- **Week 3** The characters in *Mr. Gumpy's Motor Car* must solve the problem of wheels stuck in the mud. Children might add a new "Fixing Problems" section to their poster: changing a tire or using a bicycle pump.

---

**Multi-age Classroom**

**Related Themes:**

**Grade 2** . . . Talent Show

**Grade 1** . . . We Can Do It!

▲

**Grade K** . . . Wheels Go Around

---

## ▶ Theme Poem: "Stop and Go"

Make a large cardboard traffic light with holes for the lights and sheets of red, yellow, and green paper attached to the back with tape hinges. Share the poem. Then have children "drive" in a circle and obey your signal as you change the lights. Add the traffic signal to your Dramatic Play Center.

STOP and GO

The traffic lights we see ahead
Are sometimes green
and sometimes red.
Red on top, and green below;
The red means STOP,
the green means GO!

Green below — GO — GO — GO!
Red on top — STOP — STOP — STOP!

by Marie Louise Allen

30

*Higglety Pigglety: A Book of Rhymes* page 30

## On-Going Project

**Materials** • toy vehicles • small household objects with wheels • video and picture books about wheels • shoeboxes, dowels, spools, pipe cleaners, buttons, toothpicks

**The Wheels Museum** Display the Theme Poster as a background for a wheels museum. Add interesting objects for investigation.

• Children can bring in toy vehicles or search for pictures of vehicles. They can tell how each one is used and how many wheels it has.
• Include "hands-on" displays with a toy tractor, a toy train engine with track, an egg beater, and an old clock, and let children investigate how the wheels or gears work.
• Provide picture books or a video about wheels. Children who are interested in special wheels (windmills, water wheels, or paddle-wheel boats) can ask parents or the librarian to help them learn more.

At the end of the theme, children can take turns being the "curator," telling classmates or parents what they have learned about wheels.

**Challenge** Put out a supply of shoeboxes, dowels, spools, pipe cleaners, and other materials, and invite small groups to build a model vehicle. They can tell about their invention and the problems they had to solve.

Wheels that Work

Our Truck

**Technology**

**www.eduplace.com**
Log onto *Education Place* for more activities relating to *Wheels Go Around*.

**Lesson Planner CD-ROM**
Customize your planning for *Wheels Go Around* with the Lesson Planner.

**Book Adventure**
**www.bookadventure.org**
This Internet reading-incentive program provides thousands of titles for students to read.

## Home Connection

Send home the theme letter for *Wheels Go Around* to introduce the theme and suggest home activities (**Blackline Master 98 or 99**).

For other suggestions relating to *Wheels Go Around,* see Home/Community Connections.

# Classroom Routines

### To introduce a routine...

1. Demonstrate the routine for the class.
2. Cycle every child through the routine at least once with supervision.
3. Establish ground rules for acceptable work products.
4. Check children's work.
5. Praise children's growing independence.

## Instructional Routines

### Phonemic Awareness: Blending Phonemes

In Theme 7's phonemic awareness activities, children blend single, separate sounds together to form words. As always, this skill category focuses on playing with sounds, not on the letters that spell those sounds.

In the basic routine outlined each day, you choose a word (from a poem or picture name) with two to four sounds, say the sounds separately, and have children blend them to say the word. At first you may need to repeat the sounds, saying them closer together. Have children whisper the word to a partner before calling it out, to ensure that every pupil responds.

Go beyond the basic activity as children's skill grows:

- Whisper one sound to each of three children. They confer to figure out the word and then say the separate sounds and the whole word for the class.
- Require a "password" before children can go to a Center or line up for recess. Using a different password for each child, say the sounds and have the child blend.
- Adapt the lyrics of "The Wheels on the Bus" for a blending game and have children supply the last line.

> **The teacher in the class says "/b//ŭ//s/."
> That's "/b//ŭ//s/," that's "/b//ŭ//s/."
> The teacher in the class says "/b//ŭ//s/,"
> And all the children say "bus, bus, bus!"**

### Phonics: Review Sounds

Are there children in your class who did not understand what you meant by "the sound for a letter" at first, or who have trouble remembering certain consonants? To help these children, a regular cycle of review is built into the routine for for every consonant lesson, in the **Compare and Review** step. Beginning with this theme, there is a second review cycle for potentially troublesome consonants: From time to time, the main lesson now reviews selected letter sounds.

## Instructional Routines (Continued)
### Phonics: Review Sounds

As you use the phonics reviews, focus on children who need extra support. For other children, these routines will confirm past learning and provide new practice. Are there children who use phonics confidently? Assign a writing task instead, with a topic or character whose name starts with the target sound.

## Management Routines
### Notes from an Alphafriend

Use the Alphafriend of the week to help you reinforce classroom rules or offer children a pat on the back. Before class, slip a hand-written note behind the Alphafriend card in the pocket chart. Allow the note to protrude a bit so that children will eventually discover it and bring it to you. The note from the "friend" can compliment children on their new skills, mention a classroom routine that could use better participation, or remind children of an upcoming event.

If children enjoy hearing from the Alphafriend, you may want to make the notes a regular feature!

You do a ducky job with those blending games!

### Teacher's Note

Some children will benefit from one-on-one work with phonemic awareness or phonics skills. Give each child a stick puppet of the Alphafriend of the week. Children can hold up their puppets as a signal to you when they need some help figuring out a new word in a story or completing a phonics page.

# Literature for Week 1

## Different texts for different purposes

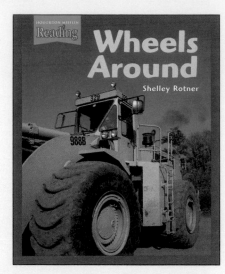

**Wheels Around**
Shelley Rotner

## Teacher Read Aloud

**Purposes**

- oral language
- listening strategy
- comprehension skill

 **Awards**

- ★ **Bank Street College Best Children's Books of the Year**
- ★ *American Bookseller's* **"Pick of the Lists"**
- ★ **Horn Book Fanfare**

## Big Books:

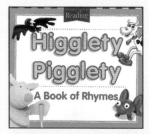

### Higglety Pigglety: A Book of Rhymes

**Purposes**

- oral language development
- phonemic awareness

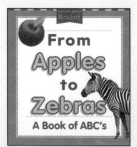

### From Apples to Zebras: A Book of ABC's

**Purposes**

- alphabet recognition
- letters and sounds

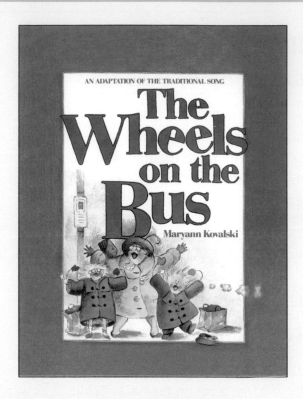

AN ADAPTATION OF THE TRADITIONAL SONG

**The Wheels on the Bus**
Maryann Kovalski

## Big Book: Main Selection

**Purposes**

- concepts of print
- reading strategy
- story language
- comprehension skills

 **Award**

- ★ **Best Books for Children**

Also available in Little Big Book and audiotape

# Leveled Books

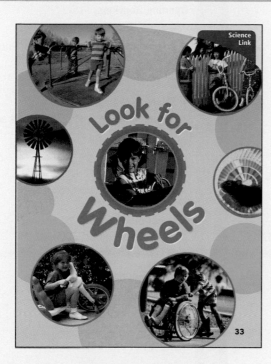

## Also in the Big Book:
## – Science Link

### Purposes

- reading strategies
- comprehension skills
- concepts of print

### Phonics Library

Also available in Take-Home version

### Purpose

- applying phonics skills and high-frequency words

## On My Way Paperback

**Dig, Zig Pig!**
*by **Sam Fonte***
page T155

### Little Readers for Guided Reading
**Collection K**

### Houghton Mifflin Classroom Bookshelf
**Level K**

### www.eduplace.com
Log on to *Education Place* for more activities relating to *Wheels Go Around*.

### www.bookadventure.org
This free Internet reading incentive program provides thousands of titles for students to read.

# Suggested Daily Routines

## Instructional Goals

### Learning to Read

✓ *Phonemic Awareness:* Blending Phonemes

*Strategy Focus:* Summarize

✓ *Comprehension Skill:* Text Organization and Summarizing

✓ *Phonics Skills*

*Phonemic Awareness:* Beginning Sound /d/

Initial Consonant *D, d;* Short *i + g*

*Compare and Review:* Initial Consonants: *f, k*

✓ *High-Frequency Word: for*

✓ *Concepts of Print:* First/Last Letter in a Word; Matching Words

### Word Work

*High-Frequency Word Practice:*
Word Families: *-ig, -it, -an*

### Writing & Language

*Vocabulary Skill:* Using Opposites

*Writing Skill:* Signs

✓ = tested skills

### 📖 Leveled Books

*Have children read in appropriate levels daily.*

**Phonics Library**
**On My Way Practice Readers**
**Little Big Books**
**Houghton Mifflin Classroom Bookshelf**

## Day 1

**Opening Routines,** *T8–T9*

[Word Wall]

• **Phonemic Awareness:** Blending Phonemes

**Teacher Read Aloud**
*Wheels Around, T10–T11*
• **Strategy:** Summarize
• **Comprehension:** Text Organization and Summarizing

### Phonics
**Instruction**
• Phonemic Awareness, Beginning Sound /d/, *T12–T13; Practice Book, 195–196*

**High-Frequency Word Practice**
• Words: *a, and, go, I, see, to, T14*

**Oral Language**
• Using Opposites, *T15*

### Managing Small Groups
**Teacher-Led Group**
• Reread familiar **Phonics Library** selections
**Independent Groups**
• Finish *Practice Book, 193–196*
• *Phonics Center:* Theme 7, Week 1, Day 1
• Book, Writing, other Centers

## Day 2

**Opening Routines,** *T16–T17*

[Word Wall]

• **Phonemic Awareness:** Blending Phonemes

**Sharing the Big Book**
*The Wheels on the Bus, T18–T19*
• **Strategy:** Summarize
• **Comprehension:** Text Organization and Summarizing

### Phonics
**Instruction, Practice**
• Initial Consonant *d, T20–T21*
• *Practice Book, 197*

**High-Frequency Word**
• New Word: *for, T22–T23*
• *Practice Book, 198*

**High-Frequency Word Practice**
• Building Sentences, *T24*

**Vocabulary Expansion**
• Using Opposites, *T25*

### Managing Small Groups
**Teacher-Led Group**
• Begin *Practice Book, 197–198* and handwriting **Blackline Masters 160 or 186.**

**Independent Groups**
• Finish *Practice Book, 197–198* and handwriting **Blackline Masters 160 or 186.**
• *Phonics Center:* Theme 7, Week 1, Day 2
• Science, Art, other Centers

**Technology**

**Lesson Planner CD-ROM:** Customize your planning for *Wheels Go Around* with the Lesson Planner.

# Day 3

**Opening Routines,** *T26–T27*

Word Wall
- **Phonemic Awareness:** Blending Phonemes

**Sharing the Big Book**
*The Wheels on the Bus, T28–T32*
- **Strategy:** Summarize
- **Comprehension:** Text Organization and Summarizing, *T31*; *Practice Book,* 199
- **Concepts of Print:** First/Last Letter in a Word, *T30*; Matching Words, *T31*

**Phonics**
**Practice, Application**
- Consonant *d, T34–T35*

**Instruction**
- Blending *d -ig, T34–T35*; *Practice Book,* 200
- **Phonics Library:** "Big Rig," *T35*

**Building Words**
- Word Family: *-ig, T36*

✎ **Shared Writing**
- Writing About Signs, *T37*
- Viewing and Speaking, *T37*

**Managing Small Groups**
**Teacher-Led Group**
- Read **Phonics Library** selection "Big Rig"
- Write letters *I, i;* begin **Blackline Masters 165 or 191.**
- Begin *Practice Book,* 199–200

**Independent Groups**
- Finish **Blackline Masters 165 or 191** and *Practice Book,* 199–200.
- Dramatic Play, other Centers

# Day 4

**Opening Routines,** *T38–T39*

Word Wall
- **Phonemic Awareness:** Blending Phonemes

**Sharing the Big Book**
**Science Link:** "Look for Wheels," *T40–T41*
- **Strategy:** Summarize
- **Comprehension:** Text Organization and Summarizing
- **Concepts of Print:** First/Last Letter in a Word; Matching Words

**Phonics**
**Practice**
- Blending *-ig* Words, *T42–T43*; *Practice Book,* 201

**Building Words**
- Word Families: *-ig, -it, -an, T44*

✎ **Interactive Writing**
- Writing About Signs, *T45*
- Listening, Viewing, and Speaking, *T45*

**Managing Small Groups**
**Teacher-Led Group**
- Reread **Phonics Library** selection "Big Rig"
- Begin *Practice Book,* 201

**Independent Groups**
- Finish *Practice Book,* 201
- *Phonics Center:* Theme 7, Week 1, Day 4
- Writing, other Centers

# Day 5

**Opening Routines,** *T46–T47*

Word Wall
- **Phonemic Awareness:** Blending Phonemes

**Revisiting the Literature**
**Comprehension:** Text Organization and Summarizing, *T48*

**Building Fluency**
- **Phonics Library:** "Big Rig," *T49*

**Phonics**
**Review**
- Familiar Consonants; *-it, T50*

**High-Frequency Word Review**
- Words: *a, and, for, go, here, I, is, like, my, see, to, T51*; *Practice Book,* 202

**Building Words**
- Word Family: *-ig, T52*

✎ **Independent Writing**
- Journals: Favorite Type of Wheels, *T53*

**Managing Small Groups**
**Teacher-Led Group**
- Reread familiar **Phonics Library** selections
- Begin *Practice Book,* 202, **Blackline Master 36.**

**Independent Groups**
- Reread **Phonics Library** selections
- Finish *Practice Book,* 202, **Blackline Master 36.**
- Centers

# Setting up the Centers

**Management Tip** Provide a special way for children to share the results of their Center activities. Either display the finished products in the Centers, or provide time for a special presentation.

**Curious George Rides a Bike**
*by H. A. Rey*

**Sheep in a Jeep** *by Nancy Shaw*

**Truck Talk** *by Bobbi Katz*

## Phonics Center

**Materials** • Phonics Center materials for Theme 7, Week 1

This week children work make words with the letters *d, f, p,* and the word family *-ig*. They also build sentences with Word and Picture cards. Prepare materials for Days 1, 2, and 4. Cut apart the letter grids and put them in plastic bags by color. Put out the Workmats and open the Direction Chart to the appropriate day. See pages T13, T21, and T43 for this week's Phonics Center activities.

## Book Center

**Materials** • books about wheels and vehicles

Read aloud some books listed from the Theme 7 Bibliography and put them in the Book Center. Also see page T11 for this week's Book Center suggestion.

## Writing Center

**Materials** • crayons, markers • lined and unlined writing paper

In this theme, children draw and label opposites pictures. Later they create drawings of everyday signs and post appropriate signs around the classroom. See pages T15 and T45 for this week's Writing Center activities.

# Science Center

**Materials** • drawing paper • red and green crayons or markers

Children examine objects on display to look for wheels and figure out how the objects work. Then children cut out pictures of things with traditional wheels or round spinning parts and create a collage. See page T19 for this week's Science Center activity.

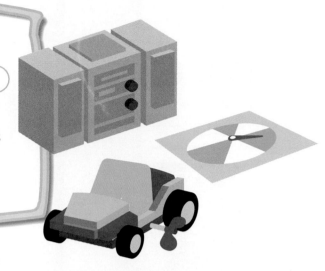

# Art Center

**Materials** • scissors • old magazines and catalogs • drawing paper • markers or crayons

Provide appealing materials in colorful, sturdy containers. Children will use them to create pairs of illustrations featuring red as *stop* and green as *go*. See page T25 for this week's Art Center activity.

stop  go

back  forth

on  off

cry  laugh

sit  stand

# Dramatic Play Center

**Materials** • chairs • dolls • packages • construction paper • crayons and markers

Children create a bus by lining up chairs with a special seat in front for the bus driver. They make traffic signs and bus safety signs. Small groups reenact *The Wheels on the Bus* or create their own story of a bus ride. See page T33 for this week's Dramatic Play Center activity.

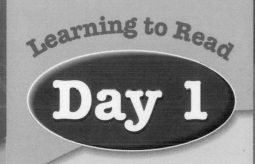

## Learning to Read

# Day 1

## Day at a Glance

### Learning to Read

**Read Aloud:**

*Wheels Around*

 **Learning About / d /, page T12**

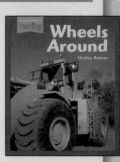

### Word Work

**High-Frequency Word Practice, page T14**

### Writing & Language

**Oral Language, page T15**

---

 **Half-Day Kindergarten**

Indicates lessons for tested skills. Choose additional activities as time allows.

---

# Opening

## Calendar

| Sunday | Monday | Tuesday | Wednesday | Thursday | Friday | Saturday |
|--------|--------|---------|-----------|----------|--------|----------|
|        |        | 1       | 2         | 3        | 4      |          |
| 🚗     | 6      | 7       | 8         | 9        | 10     | 11       |
| 12     | 13     | 14      | 15        | ✖        | 17     | 18       |
| 19     | 20     | 21      | 22        | 23       | 24     | 25       |
| 26     | 🚌     | 28      | 29        | 30       | 31     |          |

Tie the calendar routine into the theme. Use vehicle-shaped labels to mark special events. For example, a school bus could be used to mark the date of a class trip or an airplane could mark a visit from someone's favorite aunt.

## Daily Message

**Modeled Writing** Incorporate high-frequency words into the daily message. Call on volunteers to spell these words for you as you write.

Bus 10 is here now.
It got stuck today!

Have children clap to the spelling of each word on the wall today: *t-o* spells *to; a-n-d* spells *and; h-e-r-e* spells *here*.

## Daily Phonemic Awareness
### Blending Phonemes

- Read "Stop and Go" on page 30 of *Higglety Pigglety*.

- Remind children that words are made up of sounds. *I'll say some sounds. You put them together to make words from the poem:* /r//ĕ//d/ (red); /g//ō/ (go); /t//ŏ//p/ (top).

- Continue the game with other one-syllable words from the poem.

**STOP and GO**

The traffic lights we see ahead
Are sometimes green
and sometimes red.
Red on top, and green below;
The red means STOP,
the green means GO!

Green below — GO — GO — GO!
Red on top — STOP — STOP — STOP!

by Marie Louise Allen

30

*Higglety Pigglety: A Book of Rhymes*, page 30

# Getting Ready to Learn

**To help plan their day, tell children that they will**

- listen to a story called *Wheels Around*.

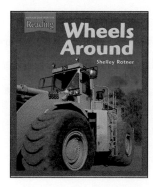

- meet a new Alphafriend, Dudley Duck.

- read, write, and learn about wheels in the Centers.

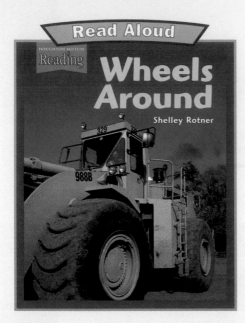

**Read Aloud**

HOUGHTON MIFFLIN
Reading

# Wheels Around
### Shelley Rotner

**Purpose** • oral language • listening strategy • comprehension skill

### Selection Summary
This photo essay shows how useful wheels are and explains what different vehicles do.

### Key Concepts
Kinds of wheels

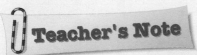
### Teacher's Note

**Read Aloud Tip**

Children may recognize many of the vehicles from their own experiences. Allow time for children to enjoy and comment on the photographs.

# Teacher Read Aloud
## Oral Language/Comprehension

▶ ## Building Background

Display *Wheels Around*. Read aloud the title and the author's and photographer's names. Ask children to name some objects at home or in the classroom that have wheels. Talk about wheels and some of the different ways wheels are used.

### Strategy: Summarize

**Teacher Modeling**  Take a picture walk with children, and model the Summarize Strategy.

#### Think Aloud

*The cover and title often tell what a book is mostly about. I think this book is about real things with wheels. As I read, I'll notice the important things about wheels. At the end, I'll tell those things in my own words.*

### Comprehension Focus: Text Organization and Summarizing

**Teacher Modeling**  Read Aloud pages 2 and 3. Then model how to get the main idea from the text.

#### Think Aloud

*I was right, This book is about wheels. These pages tell me that wheels help us work and play. I'll remember: wheels for work and for play. Those words will help me remember the important things this book tells about wheels.*

## ▶ Listening to the Story

Point to the photographs as you read to help children connect the text with the photographs. Pause occasionally to help children summarize what they've read about wheels for work or play. Encourage comments and questions.

## ▶ Responding

**Summarizing the Story** Help children summarize parts of the story.

- ■ *What are some of the ways wheels work for us? help us play?*

- ■ *What kinds of wheels help us get around? Which help keep us safe?*

- ■ *Which "wheels" were your favorite? Why?*

**Practice Book pages 193–194** Children will complete the pages at small group time.

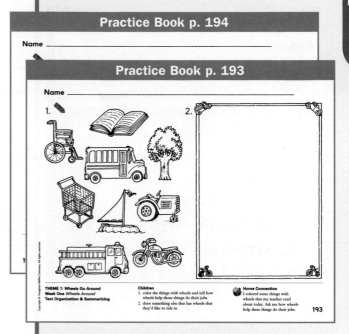

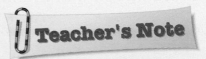

**Teacher's Note**

You may wish to post an illustrated list of the vehicles from the story in the Writing Center. This will help children who want to use the words in their writing and remind them of the different ways wheels help us.

### At Group Time

## Book Center

Make sure your Book Center is filled with books about many different kinds of wheels. Titles like *Curious George Rides a Bike* by H. A. Rey, *Sheep in a Jeep* by Nancy Shaw, *Wheels!* by Annie Cobb, *Window Music* by Anastasia Suen, and *Seymour Simon's Book of Trucks* are some good choices for the Center.

## OBJECTIVES

**Children**

- identify pictures whose names begin with /d/

## MATERIALS

- **Alphafriend Cards** *Dudley Duck, Fifi Fish, Keely Kangaroo*
- **Alphafriend Audiotape** Theme 7
- **Alphafolder** *Dudley Duck*
- **Picture Cards** for *d, f,* and *k*
- **Phonics Center:** Theme 7, Week 1, Day 1

### Home Connection

A take-home version of Dudley Duck's song is on an **Alphafriend Blackline Master.** Children can share the song with their families.

# Phonemic Awareness
## ✓ *Beginning Sound*

### ▶ Introducing the Alphafriend: Dudley Duck

Use the Alphafriend routine below to introduce Dudley Duck.

**1 Alphafriend Riddle** Read these clues:

- *This Alphafriend is an animal. His sound is /d/. Say it with me: /d/.*
- *This Alphafriend has feathers called down.*
- *He swims and dives for his dinner. He makes quacks!*

When most hands are up, call on children until they guess *duck.*

**2 Pocket Chart** Display Dudley Duck in the pocket chart. Say his name, exaggerating the /d/ sound slightly. Have children echo you.

**3 Alphafriend Audiotape** Play Dudley Duck's song. *Listen for words that start with /d/.*

**4 Alphafolder** Have children look at the scene and name all the /d/ pictures.

**5 Summarize**

- *What is our Alphafriend's name? What is his sound?*
- *What words in our Alphafriend's song start with /d/?*
- *Each time you look at Dudley this week, remember the /d/ sound.*

### Dudley Duck Song
(tune:"My Bonnie Lies over the Ocean")

Oh, look at the dandy duck, Dudley.
Dudley will dig all day long.
Dudley will dive in the water.
And Dudley will dance to this song.

## ▶ Listening for / d /

**Compare and Review: / f /, / k /** Display Alphafriends *Fifi Fish* and *Keely Kangaroo* opposite *Dudley Duck.* Review each character's sound.

Hold up the Picture Cards one at a time. Children signal "thumbs up" for pictures that start with Dudley Duck's sound, / d /, and a volunteer puts the card below Dudley's picture. For "thumbs down" words, volunteers put cards below the correct Alphafriends.

Pictures: *dog, fan, kite, fork, desk, key, doll, king, fox*

Tell children they'll sort more pictures in the Phonics Center today.

## ▶ Listening for / d /

**Practice Book pages 195–196** Children will complete the pages at small group time.

### At Group Time

# Phonics Center

Use the Phonics Center materials for **Theme 7, Week 1, Day 1.**

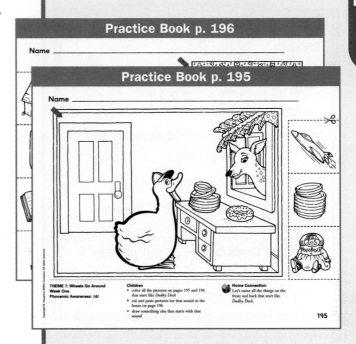

Practice Book p. 196

Name

Practice Book p. 195

Name

THEME 7: Wheels Go Around
Week One
Phonemic Awareness: /d/

Children
• color all the pictures on pages 195 and 196 that start like *Dudley Duck*
• cut and paste pictures for that sound in the boxes on page 196
• draw something else that starts with that sound

Home Connection
Let's name all the things on the front and back that start like *Dudley Duck.*

195

# Day 1

## OBJECTIVES

**Children**

- read high-frequency words
- create and write sentences with high-frequency words

## MATERIALS

- **Word Cards** *a, and, go,l, see, to, a*
- ***Higglety Pigglety: A Book of Rhymes,*** page 30
- **Picture Cards** *farm, goat, lion, pig, seal, zoo*
- **Punctuation Card:** period

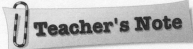

## Teacher's Note

You will also ned a word card for *can* to build the sample sentences.

## ▶ Matching Words

- Display Word Cards for the high-frequency words *I, see, and, go, to, and, a* in a pocket chart. Call on children to identify each word and to match it on the Word Wall.

- Remind children that they will see these words often in books. **I'll read a poem. You listen to hear if these words are in it.**

- Read "Stop and Go" on page 30 of *Higglety Pigglety.* **Did you hear some of these words in the poem? I did. Let's see which Word Cards you can match to the words in the poem.** (see, and, go)

**Higglety Pigglety: A Book of Rhymes,** page 30

✏️ **Writing Opportunity** Display *I, to, go, a,* and add Picture Cards for *farm, zoo, goat, pig, lion,* and *seal.* Make a word card for *can* and help children read it. Ask volunteers to use some of the cards to make sentences. Continue, adding the cards *see, and.* Children can then choose a sentence, write it, and add their own drawings.

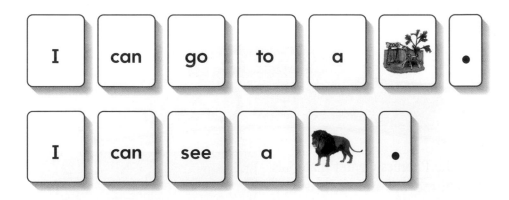

# Oral Language

▶ **Using Opposites**

■ Display and read page 6 of *Wheels Around*. Have children identify the *old* car and the *new* car on the page. Explain that words like *old* and *new* are called opposites. Write the words on chart paper.

■ Continue the list by citing other story vehicles. **Tow trucks pull cars. What is the opposite of pull? Cherry pickers lift things up. What is the opposite of up?**

■ Use a puppet to help children brainstorm opposites. Put the puppet *in* a box, then take it *out*. Put it *under* a table, then *on*.

■ Read words on the chart and have children use them in oral sentences about objects in the classroom.

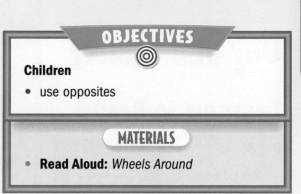

**OBJECTIVES**

**Children**
• use opposites

**MATERIALS**

• **Read Aloud:** *Wheels Around*

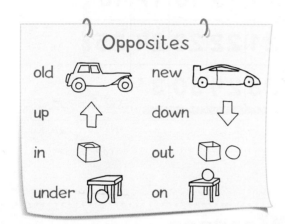

**At Group Time**

# Writing Center

Put the chart in the Writing Center and ask children to draw their own opposites pictures. They can label their drawings, copying words from the chart or using temporary phonics spellings.

## Learning to Read
# Day 2

# Day at a Glance

## Learning to Read

**Big Book:**

*The Wheels on the Bus*

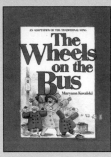

☑ **Phonics:** Initial Consonant *d*, *page T20*

☑ **High-Frequency Word:** *is*, *page T22*

## Word Work

**High-Frequency Word Practice,** *page T24*

## Writing & Language

**Vocabulary Expansion,** *page T25*

 **Half-Day Kindergarten**

☑ Indicates lessons for tested skills. Choose additional activities as time allows.

# Opening

## Calendar

| Sunday | Monday | Tuesday | Wednesday | Thursday | Friday | Saturday |
|--------|--------|---------|-----------|----------|--------|----------|
|  |  |  | 1 | 2 | 3 | 4 |
| 5 | 6 | 7 | 8 | 9 | 10 | 11 |
| 12 | 13 | 14 | 15 | 16 | 17 | 18 |
| 19 | 20 | 21 | 22 | 23 | 24 | 25 |
| 26 | 27 | 28 | 29 | 30 | 31 |  |

Thursday will be sunny.

Share and discuss weather forecasts with children. Post what the weather is expected to be later in the week and have children check the weather when that day arrives.

## Daily Message

**Modeled Writing** Write about something that happened yesterday. Compare yesterday and today on the calendar. Do this all week to help children with the concepts.

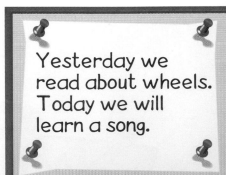

Yesterday we read about wheels. Today we will learn a song.

Today, children can take turns finding and naming Word Wall words as you spell them out.

## Daily Phonemic Awareness
### Blending Phonemes

- Read "To Market, To Market" on page 31 of *Higglety Pigglety*.

- Play a guessing game. *I'll say some sounds. You put them together to make words from the poem:* /p/ /ĭ/ /g/ (pig) /j/ /ŏ/ /g/ (jog) /h/ /ō/ /m/ (home).

- Continue the game with other one-syllable words.

**TO MARKET, TO MARKET**

To market, to market, to buy a fat pig,
Home again, home again, jiggety jig.
To market, to market, to buy a fat hog,
Home again, home again, jiggety jog.
To market, to market, to buy
a plum bun,
Home again, home again,
market is done.

a Mother Goose Rhyme

*Higglety Pigglety: A Book of Rhymes, page 31*

## Getting Ready to Learn

**To help plan their day, tell children that they will**

- listen to a Big Book: *The Wheels on the Bus*.

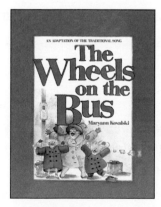

- learn the new letters *D* and *d* and their sound.

- discover ways to use wheels in the Science Center.

DAY 2

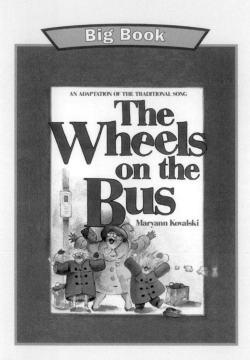

Big Book

AN ADAPTATION OF THE TRADITIONAL SONG
**The Wheels on the Bus**
Maryann Kowalski

**Purposes** • concepts of print • story language
• reading strategy • comprehension skill

---

**Selection Summary**
A grandmother and her grandchildren sing a song about a bus as they wait at a bus stop.

**Key Concepts**
City buses, taxis
Waiting for a bus

---

**MEETING INDIVIDUAL NEEDS**

**English Language Learners**

Teach children to sing "The Wheels on the Bus." Sing the first verse through once. Then sing it slowly, making sure children can hear the individual words. When children are ready, have them join in. Then ask children to listen for the words to the song as you read the story.

---

# Sharing the Big Book
## Oral Language/Comprehension

▶ **Building Background**

Read the Big Book title and the author/illustrator's name. Ask if children have ever sung "The Wheels on the Bus." Sing the first verse together or have volunteers sing for the class. Explain that part of this story includes the song. Then have children tell what they know about buses.

*Wheels Around was an information book about real wheels. But today's book tells a story about made-up characters.* Identify Grandma, Jenny, and Joanna on the cover.

**Strategy: Summarize**

**Teacher Modeling**  Model the Summarize Strategy:

**Think Aloud**

• *I know that when I read a story, I should pay attention to different things than when I read an information book like* Wheels Around. *With a story, I think about where the story takes place, who the characters are, and what happens to them. Let's do that with* The Wheels on the Bus.

**Comprehension Focus:
Text Organization and Summarizing**

**Teacher Modeling**  Tell children that thinking about the topic and main idea can help them to remember new things.

**Think Aloud**

*Part of this story gives information about something in real life: a city bus. When I get to that part, I'll look for all the things that happen on a bus ride. Let's see what we can learn about real buses.*

## ▶ Sharing the Story

Track the print as you read the selection aloud, emphasizing the rhythm and language pattern. On the pages from the song, pause to let children complete or supply phrases and ask what they have learned about a city bus.

## ▶ Responding

**Personal Response** Encourage children to use the language of the story as they react to it.

■ *Were you surprised by the ending? Did you laugh? Do you think it was a good idea for Grandma, Joanna, and Jenny to take a taxi? Why?*

■ *Do you think singing is a fun way to pass the time? What else could people do while waiting?*

■ *What sounds do the wipers on the bus make? the horn? What was your favorite "bus" sound?*

**At Group Time**

Materials • old magazines and catalogs • drawing paper • crayons

Display items that have wheels or rotating parts. Include such things as an egg beater, wind-up toy, radio with knobs, and a game spinner as well as toy trucks and cars. Encourage children to examine the items and look for parts that turn. Then they can look for magazine pictures of things with wheels or rotating parts and cut them out for a collage.

 **Extra Support**

Reinforce the concept of opposites by having children sing along and add motions as you reread the story. They can move *back* and *forth* for the wipers, hop *on* and *off* the bus, and go *up* and *down* as passengers.

**Extra Support**

To help children remember the sound for *d*, point out that the letter's name gives a clue to its sound: *d, /d/.*

# Phonics

## ✓ Initial Consonant d

### ▶ Develop Phonemic Awareness

**Beginning Sound** Read aloud the lyrics to Dudley Duck's song and have children echo it line-for-line. Have them listen for the /d/ words and "duck" their heads for each one they hear.

### Dudley Duck's Song

(Tune: "My Bonnie Lies over the Ocean")

Oh, look at the dandy duck, Dudley.
Dudley will dig all day long.
Dudley will dive in the water.
And Dudley will dance to this song.

### ▶ Connect Sounds to Letters

**Beginning Letter** Display the *Dudley Duck* card, and have children name the letter on the picture. Say: *The letter* d *stands for the sound /d/, as in* duck. *When you seen a* d, *remember* Dudley Duck. *That will help you remember the sound /d/.*

Write *duck* on the board. Underline the *d*. *This is the word* duck. *What is the first letter in the word?* (d) Duck *starts with /d/, so* d *is the first letter I write for* duck.

**Compare and Review: *p, r*** In the pocket chart, display the Letter Cards as shown and the Picture Cards in random order. Review the sounds for *d, p,* and *r*. Have children take turns naming a picture, saying its beginning sound, and putting the card below the right letter.

Tell children they will sort more pictures today in the Phonics Center.

## ▶ Handwriting

**Writing _D_, _d_** Tell children that now they'll learn to write the letters that stand for /d/: capital _D_ and small _d_. Write each letter on the letter cards as you recite the handwriting rhymes. Children can chant each rhyme as they "write" the letters in the air.

### Handwriting Rhyme: D

Big _D_ starts with a
long line down.
Go back to the top and
curve all the way around:
It's a _D_, a big _D_!

### Handwriting Rhyme: d

Start in the middle.
Make a circle nice and round.
Go up to the top and
come straight down:
It's a _d_, a small _d_!

## ▶ Apply

**Practice Book page 197** Children will complete the page at small group time.

**Blackline Master 160** This page provides additional handwriting practice for small group time.

### At Group Time

## Phonics Center

Use the Phonics Center materials for **Theme 7, Week 1, Day 2**.

### Practice Book p. 197

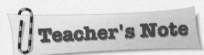

Name _____

197

THEME 7: Wheels Go Around
Week One
Phonics: Initial Consonant _d_

Children
• for 1 and 2, practice writing _Dd_ and then write _d_ beside the pictures whose names start like _Dudley Duck_
• for 3, draw two things whose names begin with _d_

Home Connection
Next time we watch TV together, let's see how many things beginning with _d_ we can find. Would you write what we find?

### ⎘ Teacher's Note

Handwriting practice for the continuous stroke style is available on **Blackline Master 186.**

### Portfolio Opportunity

Occasionally save handwriting samples for children's portfolios to show growth over time.

## Learning to Read

# Day 2

# High-Frequency Word

*New Word:* for

### OBJECTIVES

**Children**
- read and write the high-frequency word *for*

### MATERIALS

- **Word Cards** *A, a, is, for*
- **Picture Cards** *bed, dog, leash, jam, jar, quilt*
- **Punctuation Card:** *period*
- ***Higglety Pigglety: A Book of Rhymes***

## ▶ Teach

Tell children that today they will learn to read and write a word that they will often see in stories. Say *for* and use it in context.

This ball is *for* my dog.    I am late *for* dinner.    This letter is *for* you.

Make sure children understand that the word *for* is different from the word and numeral *four*. Have volunteers use *for* in oral sentences.

Write *for* on the board, and have children spell it as you point to the letters. Say: **Spell for with me, f-o-r, for.** Lead children in a chant, clapping on each beat, to help them remember the spelling: **f-o-r, for! f-o-r, for!**

**Word Wall** Post *for* on the Word Wall, and remind children to look there when they need to remember how to write the word.

## ▶ Practice

**Reading** Build the following sentences in the pocket chart. Children take turns reading. Place the pocket chart in the Phonics Center so that children can practice building and reading sentences.

Display page 16 of *Higglety Pigglety.*

■ Share the rhyme "Baa, Baa, Black Sheep."

■ Reread the last four lines of the poem, tracking the print and asking children to listen for the word *for*. Then ask children to point to *for* each time it appears.

Baa, Baa, Black Sheep

Baa, baa, black sheep,
Have you any wool?
Yes, sir, yes, sir,
Three bags full,
One for the master,
One for the dame,
One for the little boy
Who lives in the lane.

a Mother Goose Rhyme

16

*Higglety Pigglety: A Book of Rhymes,* **page 16**

▶ **Apply**

**Practice Book page 197** Children will read and write *for* as they complete the Practice Book page. On Day 3, they will practice reading *for* in the **Phonics Library** story "Big Rig."

**Practice Book p. 197**

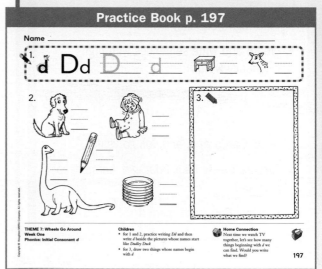

Diagnostic Check

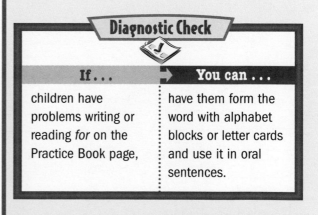

| If . . . | You can . . . |
|---|---|
| children have problems writing or reading *for* on the Practice Book page, | have them form the word with alphabet blocks or letter cards and use it in oral sentences. |

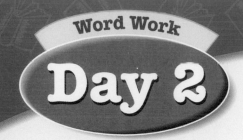
# High-Frequency Word Practice

▶ **Building Sentences**

Tell children that you want to build a sentence about things with wheels.

## OBJECTIVES

**Children**

- read high-frequency words
- create and write sentences with high-frequency words

## MATERIALS

- **Word Cards** A, a, and, for, go, is, to
- **Picture Cards** bike, boat, girl, horse, jeep, man, van
- **Punctuation Card:** period

- Display the Word and Picture Cards in random order. Then put the cards for *A* and *van* in the pocket chart and read: **A van.**

- *I want the next word to be* is. *Who can find that word? Now who can read my sentence so far?*

- Continue building the sentence: *A van is for a man and a girl.* Read the completed sentence together.

- Children can replace *van, man,* and *girl* with other cards and read their new sentences.

**Writing Opportunity** Children can write their own sentences based on one above. They might use their own names, substitute "wheels" of their own choosing, and add drawings. If children want to add new words, remind them to use what they know about letter sounds to spell the words (temporary phonics spellings).

A bike is for me.

# Vocabulary Expansion

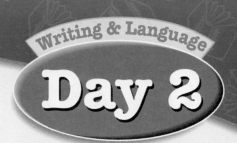
## ▶ Using Opposites

**Viewing and Speaking** Display the opposites chart children began yesterday and briefly review it.

- Ask if children can think of opposites from *The Wheels on the Bus* to add to the chart. Page through the book for ideas from the pictures.

- Add children's suggestions to the chart. Whenever possible, have them dramatize the words.

DAY 2

### OBJECTIVES

**Children**
- name some opposites

### Challenge

Some children will think of other opposites to add to the chart. Challenge them to think of a single object that performs opposite actions. For example, wipers and swings go back and forth, seesaws and elevators go up and down, and lights go on and off. Children can draw and label pictures to show their ideas.

### At Group Time

## Art Center

**Materials** • drawing paper • red and green crayons or markers

Explain that red and green are not opposites, but that the colors *red* and *green* stand for the opposites *stop* and *go*. Write these words on separate sheets of red and green paper and place them in the Art Center. Children can create pairs of illustrations with a red label for *stop* (or *danger*) and a green one for *go*.

### English Language Learners

Although English language learners may not know both words in an opposite pair, they will know some words that have opposites. Encourage children to name words and have their English-speaking classmates provide the opposite.

# Day 3

## Day at a Glance

### Learning to Read

**Big Book:**

*The Wheels on the Bus*

☑ **Phonics: Blending d -ig,** page T34

### Word Work

**Building Words,** *page T36*

### Writing & Language

**Shared Writing,** *page T37*

---

**Half-Day Kindergarten**

☑ Indicates lessons for tested skills. Choose additional activities as time allows.

---

# Opening

## Calendar

| Sunday | Monday | Tuesday | Wednesday | Thursday | Friday | Saturday |
|--------|--------|---------|-----------|----------|--------|----------|
| | | | 1 | 2 | 3 | 4 |
| 5 | 6 | 7 | 8 | 9 | 10 | 11 |
| 12 | 13 | 14 | 15 | 16 | 17 | 18 |
| 19 | 20 | 21 | 22 | 23 | 24 | 25 |
| 26 | 27 | 28 | 29 | 30 | 31 | |

Recite the days of the week with children. Frame *Monday* and call on a volunteer to find the letter *d*. Say *Monday*, asking children to listen for / d /. Repeat for the other days of the week. Frame the word *day* in each day's name.

## Daily Message

**Modeled Writing** Try to use *d* words in the daily message. Call on volunteers to point to and circle each d. Help children see that letters, like *d*, can appear in the beginning, the middle, or the end of a word, as in the sample shown.

Today we will design signs.

## Word Wall

Choose a volunteer to point to and read the new word that was added to the wall this week. *(for)* Have children compare *for* to other words on the wall. For example: *for* has three letters like *see* and *and; for* has an *o* like *to* and *go.* Continue reading the remaining groups of words.

# Routines

## Daily Phonemic Awareness
### Blending Phonemes

- Read "Hey, Diddle, Diddle" on page 32 of *Higglety Pigglety*.

- Tell children that they can play "Pat, Pat, Clap" to name different things in the poem. Review that in "Pat, Pat, Clap" children pat for each sound you say and then clap to say the word.

- Begin with words having two sounds: /h/ /ā/ (hey); /k/ /ow/ (cow); /s/ /ē/ (see).

- Continue with three pats for words having three sounds: /d/ /ŏ/ /g/ (dog); /c/ /ă/ /t/ (cat); /r/ /ă/ /n/ (ran); /d/ /ĭ/ /sh/ (dish).

**Hey, Diddle, Diddle**

Hey, diddle, diddle!
The cat and the fiddle,
The cow jumped over the moon.
The little dog laughed
To see such sport,
And the dish ran away
With the spoon.

a Mother Goose Rhyme

32

*Higglety Pigglety: A Book of Rhymes*, page 32

## Getting Ready to Learn

**To help plan their day, tell children that they will**

- reread and talk about the Big Book: *The Wheels on the Bus.*

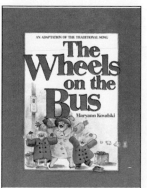

- read a story called "Big Rig."

**Big Rig**
by Amy Griffin
illustrated by Bob Kolar

- take a bus ride in the Dramatic Play Center.

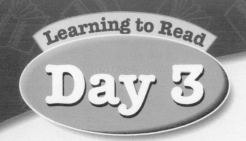

# Day 3

# Sharing the Big Book

**Children**

- identify text organization and summarize text
- identify the first and last letters of a written word

**Big Book**

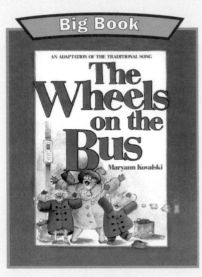

AN ADAPTATION OF THE TRADITIONAL SONG
**The Wheels on the Bus**
Maryann Kovalski

**Reading for Understanding** Reread the story, emphasizing the rhythm. Pause for discussion points.

**Extra Support**

Help children see that this book is a story within a story. There is the story of Grandma, Jenny and Joanna shopping, waiting for the bus, singing, and missing the bus. The second story takes place on the bus, during the song. Take a picture walk of this story to help children understand the sequence of events.

One day, Grandma took Jenny and Joanna shopping for new winter coats.

**pages 2–3**

They tried on long coats and short coats, blue coats and red coats, plaid coats and even raincoats.

Joanna chose a coat with wooden barrel buttons. Jenny liked it too, because of the hood.

**pages 4–5**

When it was time to go home, the bus didn't come for a long time and everyone grew tired. "I have an idea, sweeties," said Grandma. "Let's sing a song my Granny sang with me when I was a little girl." And so they began to sing. . . .

**pages 6–7**

The wheels on the bus go
round and round
round and round
round and round

The wheels on the bus go
round and round
all around the town.

8          9

**pages 8–9**

The wipers on the bus go
swish, swish, swish
swish, swish, swish
swish, swish, swish
The wipers on the bus go
swish, swish, swish
all around the town.

10          11

**pages 10–11**

The people on the bus hop
on and off
on and off
on and off
The people on the bus hop
on and off
all around the town.

12          13

**pages 12–13**

## ▶ Supporting Comprehension

**pages 4–5**

**Drawing Conclusions**

■ *Do the girls buy the first coats they try on? Why do you think that?* (No. Coats are piled on the floor; the salesclerk looks tired.)

**pages 6–7**

### Strategy: Summarize

**Teacher-Student Modeling** Review that to retell a story, readers think about the characters, where the story takes place, and what happens. Prompts:

■ *Who is the story about? Where are Grandma, Jenny, and Joanna when the story starts?* (shopping) *Where are they now?* (at the bus stop) *How do they pass the time?* (They sing.)

**pages 8–9**

### ✓ Comprehension Focus: Text Organization and Summarizing

**Teacher-Student Modeling** Point to the picture. Say: *This page begins the part of the story that tells what happens on the bus ride. What can you learn about a bus from these pages? Let's see what else we can learn.*

**pages 10–11**

**Cause and Effect**

■ *What part of the bus did we read about here? Why do the wipers swish?*

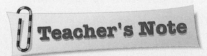

### Teacher's Note

Pages 8 and 9 show Piccadilly Circus in London, England. Point out the double-decker buses, which may be unfamiliar to children.

**DAY 3**

▶ ## Supporting Comprehension

**pages 14–15**

**Drawing Conclusions**

- *Are the people enjoying the ride? How do you know?* (Yes. They are smiling.) *Why might the driver toot his horn?* (to warn people to get out of the way)

**pages 18–19**

**Cause/Effect**

- *Why did the people go up and down?* (Perhaps the bus hit a bump or the driver stopped suddenly.) *Do you think the people should have been standing in the aisle? Why or why not?*

**pages 20–21**

✓ ## Comprehension Focus: Text Organization and Summarizing

**Student Modeling** Ask what else children have learned about these old-fashioned buses. (Equipment: wheels, wipers, a horn) *What job do buses do?* (take people where they want to go)

**Revisiting the Text**

**pages 18–19**

## Concepts of Print

✓ **First/Last Letter in a Word**

- Frame the word *and* and read it aloud. *How many letters are in this word?* (three) *What is the first letter? the last? How do you know where the word ends?* (There is a space after it.) Repeat with the words *bus* and *town.*

The horn on the bus goes
toot, toot, toot
toot, toot, toot
toot, toot, toot
The horn on the bus goes
toot, toot, toot
all around the town.

14   15

**pages 14–15**

The money on the bus goes
clink, clink, clink
clink, clink, clink
clink, clink, clink
The money on the bus goes
clink, clink, clink
all around the town.

16   17

**pages 16–17**

The people on the bus go
up and down
up and down
up and down
The people on the bus go
up and down
all around the town.

18   19

**pages 18–19**

The babies on the bus go
waaa, waaa, waaa
waaa, waaa, waaa
waaa, waaa, waaa
The babies on the bus go
waaa, waaa, waaa
all around the town.

20                                                      21

**pages 20–21**

The parents on the bus go
ssh, ssh, ssh
ssh, ssh, ssh
ssh, ssh, ssh
The parents on the bus go
ssh, ssh, ssh
all around the town.

22                                                      23

**pages  22–23**

The wheels on the bus go
round and round
round and round
round and round
The wheels on the bus go
round and round
all around the town.

24

Grandma, Jenny, and
Joanna had so much fun . . .

25

**pages 24–25**

▶ **Supporting Comprehension**

**page 20–21**

**Making Judgments**

■ *Are the people still enjoying their ride?*
*Why not?* (Babies are crying; people are frowning.)
*Would you like to be on the bus now?*

**pages 24–25**

**Drawing Conclusions**

■ *What is happening now?* (The story goes back to
Grandma and the girls.)

**pages 24–25**

 **Comprehension Focus: Text
Organization and Summarizing**

**Student Modeling** *What have you learned
about buses in this part of the story?*

**Revisiting the Text**

**pages 24–25**

**Concepts of Print**

**Matching Words**

■ Frame and read *bus*. Have volunteers match
*bus* elsewhere on the page. **Matching words
are spelled the same way.** Frame and spell
*bus* each time it appears. Repeat with
*round*.

 **Challenge**

Children who can easily match words in the text
may be able to find and match phrases that
repeat, such as "round and round." At small group
time, have these children find matching phrases.

**Sharing the Big Book**   **T31**

DAY 3

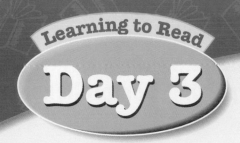

## Supporting Comprehension

**pages 26–27**

**Cause and Effect**

- *What happened because Grandma, Jenny, and Joanna were having so much fun singing?*
  (They missed the bus.)

**page 30**

**Sequence of Events**

- *What did Grandma, Jenny, and Joanna do next?*
  (took a taxi)

> **page 30**
>
> ## ✓ Strategy: Summarizing
>
> **Student Modeling** Call on volunteers to name the main characters. Ask: *What important things did Grandma, Jenny, and Joanna do at the beginning of the story?* (shopped, waited for a bus) *in the middle of the story?* (sang a song) *at the end?* (missed the bus, took a taxi)

They missed the bus!

**pages 26–27**

So . . .

**pages 28–29**

They took a taxi.

**page 30**

---

### Oral Language

**taxi:** A taxi is a car that gives you a ride somewhere. People pay the driver for taking them where they want to go. Explain how a taxi ride differs from a bus ride.

## ▶ Responding to the Story

**Retelling** Use these prompts to help children summarize the story:

■ *Why did Grandma take Jenny and Joanna shopping? Why did Grandma, Jenny, and Joanna begin singing?*

■ *What things happened on the bus in the song?*

■ *Why did Grandma, Jenny, and Joanna miss the bus? What happened at the end of the story?*

■ *What does the story tell about a real, old-fashioned bus ride?*

**Literature Circle** Have small groups discuss their favorite parts of the book. *Would you have enjoyed riding on the old-fashioned bus in the song? Why?*

**Practice Book page 199** Children will complete the page at small group time.

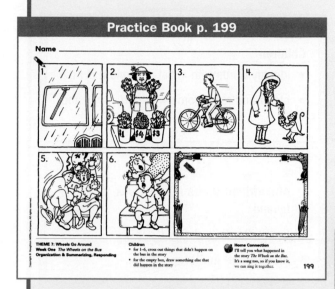
Practice Book p. 199

## Dramatic Play Center

> **Materials** • props for dramatizing the story

Set up the Dramatic Play Center to resemble a bus. Children can line up chairs for passengers and have a special seat for the driver. They can create traffic signs and bus safety signs. Provide props for riders to use on the bus, such as dolls and packages. Have small groups of children visit the center to reenact the bus ride from the story or create their own bus-ride scenario.

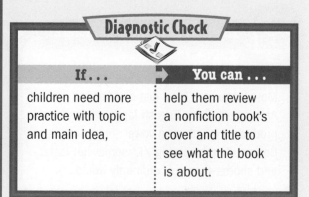

### Diagnostic Check

| If... | You can... |
|---|---|
| children need more practice with topic and main idea, | help them review a nonfiction book's cover and title to see what the book is about. |

Responding to the Story    T33

# Phonics

## ✓ *Blending* d -ig

### ▶ Connect Sounds to Letters

**Review Consonant *d*** Play Dudley Duck's song, and have children clap for each /d/ word. Write *D* and *d* on the board, and list words from the song.

**Blending *-ig*** Tell children that they'll build a word with *d*, but first they'll need a vowel ("helper letter"). Display Alphafriend *Iggy Iguana.*

*You remember Iggy. Iggy is an iguana. Say **Iggy Iguana** with me. Iggy's letter is the vowel* **i**, *and the sound* **i** *usually stands for is* /ĭ/. Hold up the Letter Card **i**. *Say* /ĭ/. *Listen for* /ĭ/ *in these words:* /ĭ/ if, /ĭ/ in, /ĭ/ itch.

Hold up the Letter Card *g* and review its sound. Tell children that they know all the letters and sounds they need to build the word *dig.* Stretch out the three sounds: /d/ /ĭ/ /g/. Build *dig* letter by letter in the pocket chart. Point to each letter and have children blend with you.

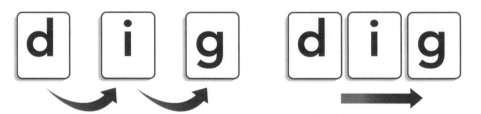

**Blending *-ig* Words** Take away the *d* and hold up Letter Card *p*. Put *p* in front of *-ig*, and model blending /p/ /ig/, *pig.* Have volunteers blend the sounds. Then blend *-ig* with familiar consonants to make *big*, *fig*, and *rig.*

**Word Wall** Add *dig* to the Word Wall. Children can use it to make words that rhyme with *dig.*

### ▶ Apply

**Practice Book page 200** Children complete the page at small group time.

---

### Practice Book p. 200

Name _____

| b | d | p |
|---|---|---|

| | i | g | Here is a _____ cat. |
| | i | g | A man can _____ . |
| | i | g | Is the _____ here? |

THEME 7: Wheels Go Around
Week One
Phonics: *d, -ig*
200

Children
- write the letters to complete the words *big, dig, pig*
- write each word to complete the sentences that go with the pictures

Home Connection
Let's cut out the letter squares on this page, mix them up, and unscramble them to build the words *pig, dig,* and *big* again.

## English Language Learners

Listen for children's pronunciation of /ĭ/. Most languages have just one *i* sound. As a result, many English language learners produce a lengthened vowel sound. Compensate by saying /ĭ/ somewhat faster and shorter than you ordinarily would.

Phonics Library

Phonics in Action

Phonics Library

Wheels Go Around

# Applying Phonics Skills and High-Frequency Words

## ▶ Introducing "Big Rig"

Do a picture walk through the first few pages of the **Phonics Library** story "Big Rig." Ask children what they think that large machine is doing.

### Phonics/Decoding Strategy

**Teacher/Student Modeling** Write the word *dig* on the board and explain that it tells what the machine likes to do. Together, use the Phonics/Decoding Strategy to read the word:

#### Think Aloud

*The word begins with d. Say the sound for d with me: /d/. We know the sounds for i, g, too: /ĭ/ /g/, -ig. Let's blend: /d/ /ig/, dig. Is dig a real word? Does it make sense when we're talking about that big machine?*

## ▶ Coached Reading

Have children read each page silently before reading with you. Prompts:

**page 1** Have volunteers model how they blended *Big* and *Rig*. **In this story, Big Rig is the name of the machine. Do you think it's a real machine? Why?**

**page 2** Together, blend *dig*. **Why do you think Big Rig is digging this hole?**

**pages 4–5** **What is Big Rig digging?** (a pit for Dan) **Why?** Have volunteers model how they blended *pit*.

**pages 6–7** **Now we know why Dan wanted a pit! What is he building?** (house with basement) Discuss why Big Rig might be digging the new hole. **What other words here rhyme with dig?** (*Big, Rig*) **What letters are the same in those rhyming words?** (*i, g,* as in *dig*)

### Phonics Library

#### Purposes
- apply phonics skills
- apply high-frequency words

**Big Rig**
by Amy Griffin
illustrated by Bob Kolar

1

Big Rig can dig.

Dig, dig, dig.

2  3

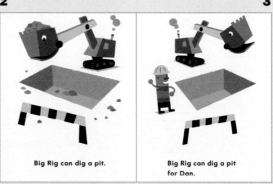

Big Rig can dig a pit.

Big Rig can dig a pit for Dan.

4  5

Dan can 🔨

Dan can ▱
Big Rig can dig.

6  7

**DAY 3**

### Home Connection

Children can color the pictures in the take-home version of "Big Rig." After rereading on Day 4, they can take it home to read to family members.

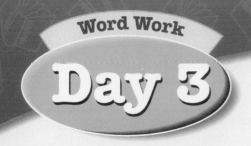

## OBJECTIVES

**Children**

• blend initial consonants with *-ig* to read words

## MATERIALS

• **Letter Cards:** *b, d, f, g, i, p, r*

# Building Words

▶ **Word Family: *–ig***

Using the Letter Cards, model how to build *dig*. *First I'll stretch out the sounds: /d/ /ĭ/ /g/. How many sounds do you hear? The first sound is /d/. I'll put up a d to spell that. The next sound is /ĭ/. What letter should I choose for that? The last sound is /g/. What letter should I choose for that?*

Blend /d/ /ĭ/ and /g/ to read *dig*. Then tell children you want to build a word that rhymes with *dig*. Replace *d* with *b* and say: *Now what happens if I change /d/ to /b/?* Continue making and blending *-ig* words by substituting *f, r,* and *p*.

Have small groups work together to build *-ig* words. They can use letter stamps or other manipulatives in your collection.

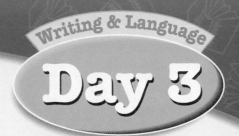
# Shared Writing

## ▶ Writing About Signs

**Viewing and Speaking** Take a brief walk around the school to observe signs. Upon returning to the classroom, help children record their observations.

- Organize these pairs of signs together on a chart, reviewing words that name opposites. Children might mention signs such as *in/out, push/pull, enter/exit,* and *boys/girls.*

- Help children brainstorm other signs they have seen. *What signs might you see when you are crossing the street? in an elevator? in a school?*

- Discuss the purposes of the signs, using prompts as needed. *Where would you see this sign? Who would read it? How would it help them?*

Use children's suggestions in a shared writing experience.

- Choose a scene to pantomime, such as driving a bus or crossing a street. Write about the event, having children suggest a sign they might see and what information it gives.

**Signs**

| | |
|---|---|
| in | out |
| enter | exit |
| walk | don't walk |
| push | pull |
| boys | girls |
| stop | go |

We are driving a bus.
We see a red sign.
It tells us to stop.

We are crossing the street.
We see a Walk sign.
It tells us we can cross safely.

**OBJECTIVES**

**Children**
- use opposites to make signs

DAY 3

**English Language Learners**

Make sure children know the meaning of signs around school and help them incorporate the words into their vocabulary. Take pictures of the signs to post in the classroom and use with children.

# Day 4

## Day at a Glance

### Learning to Read

**Big Book:**

*Look for Wheels*

☑ Phonics: Reviewing /d/; Blending -ig Words, page T42

### Word Work

**Building Words,** *page T44*

### Writing & Language

**Interactive Writing,** *page T45*

---

 **Half-Day Kindergarten**

☑ Indicates lessons for tested skills. Choose additional activities as time allows.

---

# Opening

## Calendar

| Sunday | Monday | Tuesday | Wednesday | Thursday | Friday | Saturday |
|--------|--------|---------|-----------|----------|--------|----------|
|        |        |         | 1         | 2        | 3      | 4        |
| 5      | 6      | 7       | 8         | 9        | 10     | 11       |
| 12     | 13     | 14      | 15        | 16       | 17     | 18       |
| 19     | 20     | 21      | 22        | 23       | 24     | 25       |
| 26     | 27     | 28      | 29        | 30       | 31     |          |

Incorporate opposite words into your calendar routine. *What day comes before Tuesday? What day comes after Thursday? The first day of the month was a _____. The last day of the month is a _____.*

The first day of the month was a _____.

The last day of the month is a _____.

## Daily Message

**Modeled Writing** Duplicate some of the words in the daily message. Call on volunteers to find and underline words that are the same. See the sample shown.

Today we will look for wheels.

Max will build something with wheels.

Distribute index cards for words on the Word Wall. Have children match their cards to the words on the Word Wall. After each match is made, have other children chant the spelling: **d-i-g** *spells* **dig.**

## Daily Phonemic Awareness
### Blending Phonemes

- Read aloud "To Market, To Market" on page 31 of *Higglety Pigglety*.

- Play a guessing game with children. **Let's put some sounds together to make words from the poem:** /j/ /ĭ/ /g/ (jig); /p/ /ĭ/ /g/ (pig); /f/ /ă/ /t/ (fat); /h/ /ŏ/ /g/ (hog).

- Repeat with other single-syllable words from the poem.

- Now make the game more challenging by using words that are not from the poem.

*Higglety Pigglety: A Book of Rhymes,* **page 31**

## Getting Ready to Learn

**To help plan their day, tell children that they will**

- read the Science Link: *Look for Wheels.*

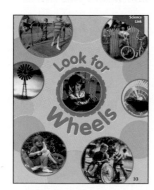

- learn to make and read new words.

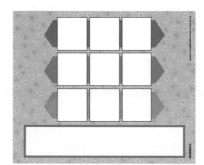

- draw and write about signs in the Writing Center.

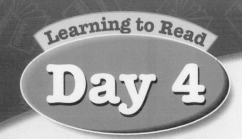

## Learning to Read
# Day 4

### OBJECTIVES

**Children**

- identify text organization
- identify the first and last letter of a written word

**Big Book**

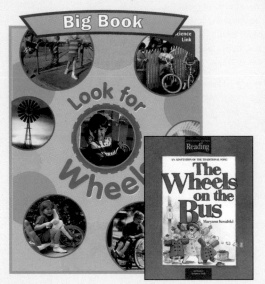

pages 33–38

## Oral Language

**fair:** Children may think of the word *fair* as meaning *just.* Explain that *fair* also names a place that has games and rides.

### English Language Learners

Help children see that the commands *look for* and *find* have similar meanings. Use both in context to demonstrate meaning: *Look for two red crayons. Find the green book.*

# Sharing the Big Book
## *Science Link*

### ▶ Building Background

*Did you see any wheels on the way to school today? Where? What did the wheels do?* Display *Look for Wheels.* Read the title aloud, and discuss the pictures on the cover. Ask children what they think this selection will be about and why.

**Reading for Understanding** Pause for discussion as you share the selection.

> **page 34**
>
> ### Strategy: Summarize
>
> **Student Modeling** Ask children what the selection has been about so far. *What have you learned about wheels?*
>
>  ### Comprehension Focus: Text Organization and Summarizing
>
> **Student Modeling** *What does the first sentence on each page tell you to do?* (look for a wheel) *Wheel is the* topic. *What does each question ask?* (what the wheel does) *What the wheel does is the important information.*

**page 34**

**Making Judgments**

*What makes this wheel turn?* (the children pushing it) *Which would you rather do, push the wheel or ride on it? Why?*

**pages 36**

**Cause and Effect**

*What makes the wheel on this page turn?* (As the hamster runs, it turns the wheel.)

**page 38**

**Compare and Contrast**

*How are wheels being used differently in each picture?*

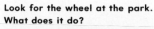

Look for the wheel at the park.
What does it do?

34

Look for the wheel inside the car.
What does it do?

35

**pages 34–35**

Look for the wheel in the cage.
What does it do?

36

Look for the wheel at the fair.
What does it do?

37

**pages 36–37**

Look for wheels around you.
What do they do?

38

**page 38**

**Revisiting the Text**

**pages 34–35**

## Concepts of Print

 **First/Last Letter of a Word; Matching Words**

■ Frame the word *for* on page 34. *How many letters are in this word? What is the first letter? The last letter?* Direct attention to page 35. *Who can match the same word on this page?* Repeat with other pairs of words.

## ▶ Responding

**Summarizing** Talk with children about the different ways wheels are used in the pictures. Have children summarize the selection, using the pictures as prompts. *What are some of the ways wheels can be used? How are all wheels alike?*

(They all turn around a center.)

**DAY 4**

 **Challenge**
MEETING INDIVIDUAL NEEDS

For children who are ready for a challenge, prepare cards for the words and end marks in one or two sentences from the selection. One child builds a sentence and then challenges a partner to read it, find it in the book, and add the correct punctuation card.

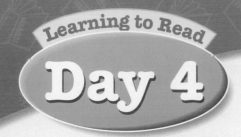

## Learning to Read

# Day 4

### OBJECTIVES

**Children**

- identify initial *d* for words that begin with / d /
- blend *d* and other initial consonants with *-ig*

### MATERIALS

- *From Apples to Zebras: A Book of ABCs* page 5
- **Alphafriend Cards** *Dudley Duck, Iggy Iguana*
- **Letter Cards**  *a, b, d, f, g, i, p, r*
- **Picture Card** *dog*
- **Punctuation Card:** *period*
- **Phonics Center:** Theme 7, Week 1, Day 4

### Teacher's Note

During writing, children may ask how to spell words from the *-ig* family. Help children find the word *dig* on the Word Wall and substitute the appropriate initial consonant(s).

### Home Connection

Challenge children to look at home for items or for names that begin with the consonant *d*. Children can draw pictures to show what they have found.

# Phonics

## *Blending -ig Words*

▶ **Connect Sounds to Letters**

**Review Consonant *d*** On page 5 of *From Apples to Zebras,* cover the words with self-stick notes. Then display the page. Ask children what letter they expect to see first in each word and why. Uncover the words so children can check their predictions.

*From Apples to Zebras: A Book of ABC's,* **page 5**

**Reviewing *-ig***
Remind children that to build words with *d*, they also need a vowel ("helper letter"), because every word has at least one of those. Ask which Alphafriend stands for the vowel sound /ĭ/. *(Iggy Iguana)* Display Iggy, and have children think of other words that start with /ĭ/. *(if, igloo, in, itch)*

Hold up Letter Cards *d, i,* and *g.* **Watch and listen as I build a word from the Word Wall: /d/ /ĭ/ /g/, dig. /d/ /ĭ/ /g/, dig.**

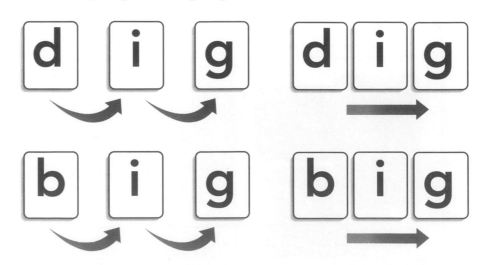

**Blending *-ig*** Remove the *d* and put the Letter Card *b* in front of *-ig.* **Now let's blend this new word: / b / / ig /, big.** Continue, having volunteers build and blend *fig, pig,* and *rig.*

## ▶ Apply

Use index cards to make word cards for *can* and *pit*. Begin a sentence with the first two cards shown. Say the words with children. For *dig*, ask what letter you need to spell each sound.

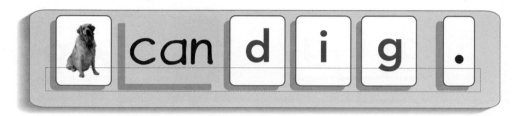

Repeat the activity with *Dog can dig a pit*. Tell children they will build more sentence in the Phonics Center.

**Practice Book page 201** Children will complete this page at small group time.

**Phonics Library** In groups today, children will also read *-at* words as they reread the **Phonics Library** story, "Big Rig." See suggestions, page T35.

**At Group Time**

# Phonics Center

Use the Phonics Center materials for **Theme 7, Week 1, Day 4**.

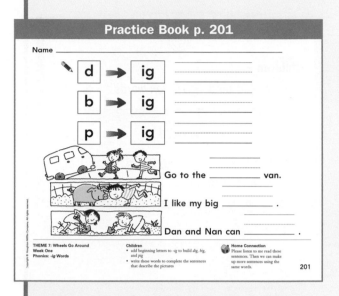
 **Portfolio Opportunity**

Save children's Practice Book pages and other writing samples for *-ig* words in their portfolios.

**DAY 4**

**MEETING INDIVIDUAL NEEDS** **Challenge**

Children who can easily build and blend *-ig* words can write additional sentences for the words *big*, *dig*, *fig*, *pig*, and *rig*.

## Diagnostic Check

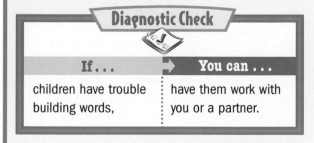

| If... | You can ... |
|---|---|
| children have trouble building words, | have them work with you or a partner. |

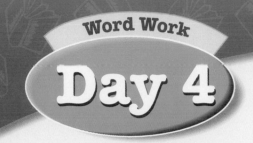
## OBJECTIVES

**Children**
- build and read -ig, -it, -an words

### MATERIALS

- **Letter Cards** *a, b, c, d, D, f, g, h, i, k, l, m, n, N, p, qu, r, s, t, v*

# Building Words

▶ **Word Families: *-ig, -it, -an***

Model how to build *dig* in the pocket chart, stretching out the sounds. ***Let's build the word* dig. *Which letter should I put first?*** Place *d* in the pocket chart. Repeat the procedure, having children supply the letters for /ĭ/ and /g/.

Next, replace the *d* with known consonants (*b, f, p, r*) to build other *-ig* words. Keep a list of words you've built.

Blend /ĭ/ and /t/ to read *it*. Ask which letter you should add to build *lit*. Model how to read *lit* by blending /l/ with /it/. Then replace *l* with *f* and say: ***Now what happens if I change /l/ to /f/?*** Continue making and blending *-it* words by substituting *b, h, k, p, qu, s*. Add the new words to your list.

Repeat for *-an* words and the initial consonants *c, D, f, m, N, p, r, t, v.*

| -ig | -it | -an |
|-----|-----|-----|
| big | bit | can |
| dig | fit | Dan |
| fig | hit | fan |
| pig | kit | man |
| rig | lit | Nan |
|     | pit | pan |
|     | quit | ran |
|     | sit | tan |
|     |     | van |

# Interactive Writing

## ▶ Writing About Signs

**Listening, Viewing and Speaking** Remind children that signs have many uses. Many help us by telling us what to do. Show children pages 6–7 of *The Wheels on the Bus*. Ask: ***How do Grandma, Jenny, and Joanna know where to wait for the bus?*** (from the "bus stop" sign)

■ Display the chart from yesterday's shared writing. (See page T37.) Review the scenes and invite children to discuss what the signs tell.

■ Continue adding sentences to the chart, for example: *We are waiting for a bus. We see a BUS STOP sign. It tells us where to stand.*

■ If a suggested word begins or ends with a known consonant, have a volunteer write the letter. Another child can write *for* or other high-frequency words. Choose someone to write the period at the end of each sentence.

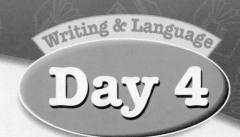

### OBJECTIVES

**Children**

● use opposites in an oral context

● write letters or words for an interactive writing activity

### MATERIALS

● **Big Book:** *The Wheels on the Bus,* pages 6–7

**Portfolio Opportunity**

Save samples of children's writing in their portfolios.

### At Group Time

## Writing Center

Put the chart paper from the previous activity in the Writing Center. Children "read" it on their own or with a partner. Each child can copy and illustrate his or her own sentence. Encourage children to show a sign in their drawings.

I stop here.

Now I can walk.

**English Language Learners**

Take pictures of signs around town to add to the school signs you photographed. (See Meeting Individual Needs note, page T37.) Encourage children to make the environmental print part of their oral and written vocabulary.

**DAY 4**

# Day 5

# Day at a Glance

## Learning to Read

**Revisiting the Literature:**

*Wheels Around, The Wheels on the Bus, Look for Wheels, "Big Rig"*

✓ **Phonics: Initial Consonants; -at, -it, -ig Words;** *page T50*

## Word Work

**Building Words,** *page T52*

## Writing & Language

**Independent Writing,** *page T53*

 **Half-Day Kindergarten**

✓ Indicates lessons for tested skills. Choose additional activities as time allows.

# Opening

## Calendar

| Sunday | Monday | Tuesday | Wednesday | Thursday | Friday | Saturday |
|--------|--------|---------|-----------|----------|--------|----------|
|        |        |         | 1         | 2        | 3      | 4        |
| 5      | 6      | 7       | 8         | 9        | 10     | 11       |
| 12     | 13     | 14      | 15        | 16       | 17     | 18       |
| 19     | 20     | 21      | 22        | 23       | 24     | 25       |
| 26     | 27     | 28      | 29        | 30       | 31     |          |

Review any words you posted on the calendar this week. Have children suggest other events to note.

## Daily Message

**Interactive Writing** As you write the daily message and model how to write letters that stand for sounds, occasionally ask volunteers to contribute words or letters they can read and write.

Brendon brought his favorite wheels to school today.

Read the Word Wall together. Then play a rhyming game: *I'm going to find a word on the wall that rhymes with sit. The word it rhymes with sit. Now raise your hand when you find a word that rhymes with big.* (dig)

# Routines

## Daily Phonemic Awareness
### Blending Phonemes

- Display Picture Cards for *dig, dog, kit, kiss, pig, pin,* and *pit.* Have children name the pictures with you.

- Remind children that words are made of small sounds. *I will say some sounds to name the mystery picture. You blend the sounds and raise your hand when you know which picture I named: /p//ĭ//g/.*

- When most hands are up, ask children to say the word aloud with you. *That's right! /p//ĭ//g/, pig.* If children mistakenly say *pin* or *pit,* say the sounds again, emphasizing the sound children need to hear to correct their mistake, for example, /g/.

- Continue until all the Picture Cards have been named. Then make the game more challenging by using words that do not name pictures.

## Getting Ready to Learn

**To help plan their day, tell children that they will**

- reread and talk about all the books they've read this week.

- take home a story they can read.

**Big Rig**
by Amy Griffin
illustrated by Bob Kolar

- write a story in their journals.

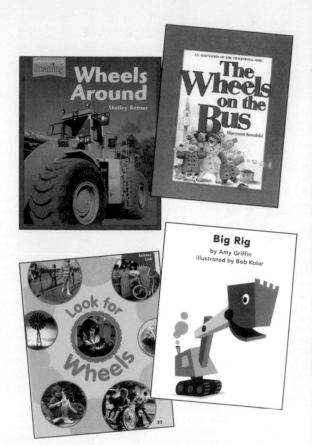

# Revisiting the Literature

........................................................

## ▶ Literature Discussion

Today children will compare the different books you shared this week: *Wheels Around, The Wheels on the Bus, Look for Wheels,* and "Big Rig." First, use these suggestions to help children recall the selections:

- Have volunteers display and tell about their favorite vehicle in *Wheels Around*.

- Sing the song from *The Wheels on the Bus*. Children can use the pictures from the book as prompts for the verses.

- Point to various photos from *Look for Wheels*. Select children to discuss what the pictured wheels do.

- Together, read "Big Rig." Ask volunteers how they blended *dig*.

- Ask children to vote for their favorite book of the week. Then read aloud winner.

## ✓ Comprehension: Text Organization and Summarizing

**Comparing Books** Remind children that the cover and title of an information book usually tell what the book is about. Explain that this is the *topic* of the book and that most of the sentences tell more about the topic. Browse through each selection with children, inviting comments about the topic and the main idea. Then help children develop a one- or two-sentence summary for each one, using the topic and main idea.

### Technology

**www.eduplace.com**

Log on to **Education Place** for more activities relating to Wheels Go Around.

**www.bookadventure.com**

This Internet reading-incentive program provides thousands of titles for children to read.

# Building Fluency

## ▶ Rereading for Fluency

**Rereading Familiar Texts**  Review **Phonics Library** books children have read so far. Remind them that they've learned the new word for this week, and that they've learned to read words with *-ig*. As they reread "Big Rig," have children look for words with *-ig*. Then feature several **Phonics Library** titles in the Book Corner, and have children demonstrate their growing skills by choosing one to reread aloud. Children can alternate pages with a partner.

**Oral Reading**  Recognizing high-frequency words by sight helps children read more smoothly. Continue to provide daily practice with words on the Word Wall. You might want to send a word list home occasionally so that children can share their growing ability to recognize words.

**Blackline Master 36**  Children complete the page and take it home to share their reading progress.

**Big Rig**
by Amy Griffin
illustrated by Bob Kolar

**Tan Van**
by Amy Griffin
illustrated by Amiko Hirao

**Zig Pig and Dan Cat**
by Amy Griffin
illustrated by Amiko Hirao

**My Reading Log**

I can read

My new words

for   dig

The materials listed below provide reading practice for children at different levels.

### Little Big Books

### Little Readers for Guided Reading

### Houghton Mifflin Classroom Bookshelf

**DAY 5**

**Home Connection**

Remind children to share the **take-home** version of "Big Rig" with their families.

# Learning to Read

## Day 5

### OBJECTIVES

**Children**

- build and read words with initial consonants and short *i* + *g*
- make sentences with high-frequency words

### MATERIALS

- **Word Cards** *a, and, for, go, here, I, is, like, my, see, to*
- **Picture Cards** *cat, dog, vet;* assorted others for sentence building
- **Punctuation Card:** period

# Phonics Review

## ✔ Consonants, Word Families

### ▶ Review

Tell children that they will take turns being word builders and word readers today. Have a group of word builders stand with you at the chalkboard.

*Let's build* dig. *First, count the sounds... . I know* /d/ *stands for* d. *I also know that* i *stands for* /ĭ/ *and* g *stands for* /g/. Write the letters.

- Children copy *dig* on the board and blend the sounds.

- At your direction, children erase the *d*, write *p* and ask the rest of the class (word readers) to say the new word.

- Continue until everyone builds a word by replacing one letter. Examples: *dig, pig, rig, fig, big; bit, sit, hit, kit, lit, pit, fit.* For a challenge, have the word builders change *fit* to *fan* and then *man, pan, ran, tan, van, can; cat, bat, fat, hat, mat, pat, rat, sat, vat.*

T50    **THEME 7: Wheels Go Around**

# High-Frequency Word Review

☑️ *a, and, for, go, here, I, is, like, my, see, to*

## ▶ Review

Give each small group the Word Cards, Picture Cards, and Punctuation Card needed to make a sentence. Remind children that the sentence begins with a capital. Children hold the cards and arrange themselves to make a sentence for others to read.

## ▶ Apply

**Practice Book page 202** Children can complete this page independently and read it to you during small group time.

**Phonics Library** Have children take turns reading aloud to the class. Each child might read one page of "Big Rig" or a favorite **Phonics Library** selection from the previous theme. Remind readers to share the pictures!

Questions for discussion:

■ *Do you hear any rhyming words in either story? What letters are the same in those words?*

■ *Find a word that starts with the same sound as Dudley Duck's name. What is the letter? What is the sound?*

■ *This week we added the word* for *to the Word Wall. Find that word in "Big Rig."*

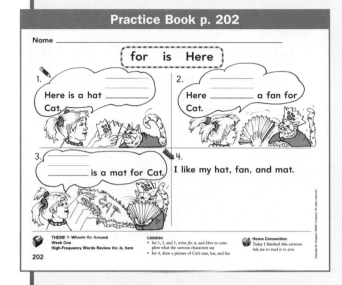

**Practice Book p. 202**

### Portfolio Opportunity

Save the **Practice Book** page to show children's recognition of high-frequency words.

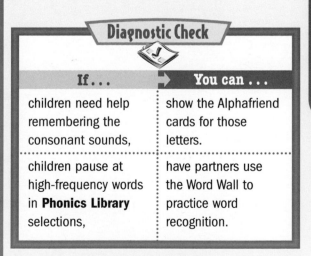

**Diagnostic Check**

| If... | You can... |
|---|---|
| children need help remembering the consonant sounds, | show the Alphafriend cards for those letters. |
| children pause at high-frequency words in **Phonics Library** selections, | have partners use the Word Wall to practice word recognition. |

**DAY 5**

## Day 5

# Building Words

▶ ## Word Families

Model how to build *dig*. Along the bottom of the pocket chart, line up the letters *f, p, r,* and *b*. **Let's build a word that rhymes with** dig. **Fig** *rhymes with* dig. **Let's build** fig. **Who can tell me which letter I should take from here to make** fig? Take away the letter *d* and have a volunteer replace it with the letter *f.* Continue building *-ig* words, using initial consonants *p, r,* and *d*. On chart paper, keep a list of all the *-ig* words you make. Reread the list together, blending the sounds.

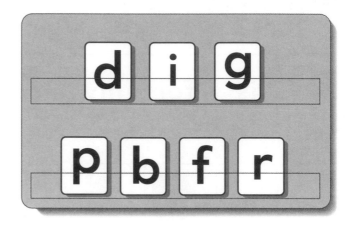

Continue the activity with *-it, -an,* and *-at* words. Examples: *dig, pig, big, fig, rig, bit, fit, hit, kit, lit, pit, sit; can, fan, man, pan, ran, tan, van; bat, cat, fat, hat, mat, pat, rat, sat, vat.*

Have small groups work together to build *-it, -an,* and *-at* words with foam letters or other manipulatives. This time, they can add new words to the Word Bank section of their journals and add appropriate pictures.

# Independent Writing

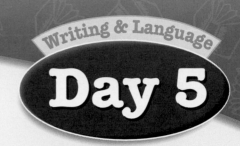

### ▶ Journals

Review what children learned about wheels so far. Point out the charts you made together, showing all the words for opposites that were used to tell about things wheels do and about signs that help people. Tell children that today they will write about their favorite type of wheels.

- Pass out the journals.

- *What are some new words about wheels or vehicles you could put in your journals? What are some opposites you might use to tell about different signs and how they help drivers?*

- Remind children that they can use words from the Word Wall and this week's charts as they write. Children can also use temporary phonics spellings for words of their own choosing.

- If time permits, allow children to share what they've written with the class.

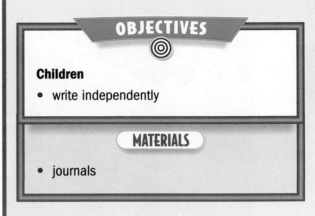

 **Teacher's Note**

Children can browse through *Wheels Around* to find the names of different vehicles to write about.

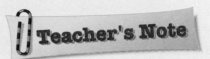 **Portfolio Opportunity**

Use self-stick notes to mark journal entries you would like to share with parents. Occasionally allow children to mark their best efforts or favorite works for sharing as well.

**DAY 5**

# Literature for Week 2

## Different texts for different purposes

*The Little Engine that Could*

## Teacher Read Aloud

### Purposes

- oral language
- listening strategy
- comprehension skill

## Big Books:

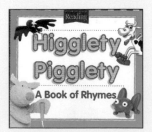

### Higglety Pigglety: A Book of Rhymes

#### Purposes

- oral language development
- phonemic awareness

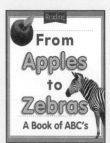

### From Apples to Zebras: A Book of ABC's

#### Purposes

- alphabet recognition
- letters and sounds

## Big Book: Main Selection

### Purposes

- concepts of print
- reading strategy
- story language
- comprehension skills

Also available in Little Big Book and audiotape

# Leveled Books

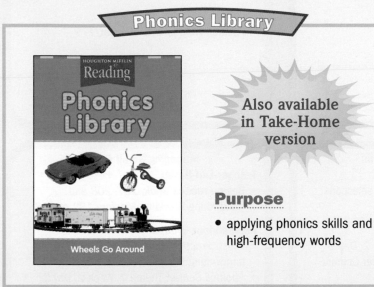

## Also in the Big Book:
## - Science Link

### Purposes

- reading strategies
- comprehension skills
- concepts of print

**Phonics Library**

Also available in Take-Home version

### Purpose

- applying phonics skills and high-frequency words

## On My Way Paperback

**Dig, Zig Pig!**
*by Sam Fonte*
page T155

## Little Readers for Guided Reading
**Collection K**

## Houghton Mifflin Classroom Bookshelf
**Level K**

**Technology**

### www.eduplace.com

Log on to *Education Place* for more activities relating to *Wheels Go Around*.

### www.bookadventure.org

This free Internet reading incentive program provides thousands of titles for students to read.

## Instructional Goals

### Learning to Read

☑ *Phonemic Awareness:* Blending Phonemes

*Strategy Focus:* Monitor/Clarify

☑ *Comprehension Skill:* Cause and Effect

☑ *Phonics Skills*

*Phonemic Awareness:* Beginning Sound /z/

Initial Consonant *Z, z;* Short *i + g*

*Compare and Review:* Initial Consonants: *p, l*

☑ *High-Frequency Word: have*

☑ *Concepts of Print:* Matching Words; Using All Capital Letters

### Word Work

*High-Frequency Word Practice:*
Word Families: *-ig, -it, -at, -an*

### Writing & Language

*Vocabulary Skills:* Using Position Words, Parts of a Car

*Writing Skill:* Writing a Class Story

☑ = tested skills

### Leveled Books

*Have children read in appropriate levels daily.*

**Phonics Library**
**On My Way Practice Readers**
**Little Big Books**
**Houghton Mifflin Classroom Bookshelf**

---

## Day 1

**Opening Routines,** *T60–T61*

**Word Wall**
• **Phonemic Awareness:** Blending Phonemes

**Teacher Read Aloud**
*The Little Engine That Could, T62–T65*
• **Strategy:** Monitor/Clarify
• **Comprehension:** Cause and Effect

### Phonics

**Instruction**
• Phonemic Awareness, Beginning Sound /z/, *T66–T67; Practice Book, 205–206*

---

**High-Frequency Word Practice**
• Words: *see, and, like, to, I, my, T68*

---

**Oral Language**
• Using Position Words, *T69*

---

**Managing Small Groups**
**Teacher-Led Group**
• Reread familiar **Phonics Library** selections

**Independent Groups**
• Finish *Practice Book, 203–206*
• *Phonics Center:* Theme 7, Week 2, Day 1
• Book, Dramatic Play, Writing, other Centers

---

## Day 2

**Opening Routines,** *T70–T71*

**Word Wall**
• **Phonemic Awareness:** Blending Phonemes

**Sharing the Big Book**
*Vroom, Chugga, Vroom-Vroom, T72–T73*
• **Strategy:** Monitor/Clarify
• **Comprehension:** Cause and Effect

### Phonics

**Instruction, Practice**
• Initial Consonant *z, T74–T75*
• *Practice Book, 207*

**High-Frequency Word**
• New Word: *have, T76–T77*
• *Practice Book, 208*

---

**High-Frequency Word Practice**
• Building Sentences, *T78*

---

**Vocabulary Expansion**
• Position Words, Parts of a Car, *T79*

---

**Managing Small Groups**
**Teacher-Led Group**
• Begin *Practice Book, 207–208* and handwriting **Blackline Masters 182 or 208.**

**Independent Groups**
• Finish *Practice Book, 207–208* and handwriting **Blackline Masters 182 or 208.**
• *Phonics Center:* Theme 7, Week 2, Day 2
• Science, Dramatic Play, other Centers

---

Technology

**Lesson Planner CD-ROM:** Customize your planning for *Wheels Go Around* with the Lesson Planner.

# Day 3

**Opening Routines,** *T80–T81*

Word Wall

- **Phonemic Awareness:** Blending Phonemes

**Sharing the Big Book**
*Vroom, Chugga, Vroom-Vroom, T82–T87*
- **Strategy:** Monitor/Clarify
- **Comprehension:** Cause and Effect, *T83;* *Practice Book,* 209
- **Concepts of Print:** Matching Words; Using All Capital Letters, *T83*

### Phonics
**Practice, Application**
- Consonant *z, T90–T91*

**Instruction**
- Blending *z -ig, T90–T91; Practice Book,* 210
- **Phonics Library:** "Tan Van," *T91*

**Building Words**
- Word Family: *-ig, T92*

✎ **Shared Writing**
- Writing a Class Story, *T93*
- Listening, *T93*

---

**Managing Small Groups**
**Teacher-Led Group**
- Read **Phonics Library** selection "Tan Van"
- Write letters *I, i;* begin **Blackline Masters 165 or 191.**
- Begin *Practice Book,* 209–210

**Independent Groups**
- Finish **Blackline Masters 165 or 191** and *Practice Book,* 209–210.
- Math, Art, other Centers

# Day 4

**Opening Routines,** *T94–T95*

Word Wall

- **Phonemic Awareness:** Blending Phonemes

**Sharing the Big Book**
**Science Link:** "Cool Wheels," *T96*
- **Strategy:** Monitor/Clarify
- **Comprehension:** Cause and Effect
- **Concepts of Print:** Match Words in Print

### Phonics
**Practice**
- Blending *-ig* Words, *T98–T99; Practice Book,* 211

**Building Words**
- Word Families: *-ig, -it, -at, T100*

✎ **Interactive Writing**
- Writing a Class Story, *T101*

---

**Managing Small Groups**
**Teacher-Led Group**
- Reread **Phonics Library** selection "Tan Van"
- Begin *Practice Book,* 211

**Independent Groups**
- Finish *Practice Book,* 211
- **Phonics Center:** Theme 7, Week 2, Day 4
- Writing, other Centers

# Day 5

**Opening Routines,** *T102–T103*

Word Wall

- **Phonemic Awareness:** Blending Phonemes

**Revisiting the Literature**
**Comprehension:** Cause and Effect, *T104*

**Building Fluency**
- **Phonics Library:** "Tan Van," *T105*

### Phonics
**Review**
- Familiar Consonants; *-at, -an, -ig, -it, T106*

**High-Frequency Word Review**
- Words: *I, see, my, like, a, to, and, go, for, have, T107; Practice Book,* 212

**Building Words**
- Word Families: *-ig, -at, -an, -it, T108*

✎ **Independent Writing**
- Journals: Trains, Race Cars, and Other Vehicles, *T109*

---

**Managing Small Groups**
**Teacher-Led Group**
- Reread familiar **Phonics Library** selections
- Begin *Practice Book,* 212, **Blackline Master 36.**

**Independent Groups**
- Reread **Phonics Library** selections
- Finish *Practice Book,* 212, **Blackline Master 36.**
- Centers

# Setting up the Centers

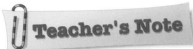

### Teacher's Note

Provide a challenge for children who complete Center activities quickly. This week, for example, invite them to draw and write about a time when, like Little Blue Engine, they tried very hard to do something and were finally successful.

Mike Mulligan and his
Steam Shovel *by Virginia Lee Burton*

Little Toot *by Hardie Gramansky*

### Phonics Center

**Materials** • Phonics Center Kit Materials for Theme 7, Week 2

This week children sort pictures for initial sounds / z /, / p /, and / l /. They make words with *b, d, p,* and the word family *-ig.* They also build sentences with Word Cards. Prepare materials for Days 1, 2, and 4. See pages T67, T75, and T99 for this week's Phonics Center activities.

### Book Center

**Materials** • books about hard-working characters that are successful

Read aloud some stories of characters that work hard and are successful. Then put copies of the books in the Book Center. See the Teacher's Note on page T63 for this week's Book Center suggestion.

### Writing Center

**Materials** • crayons, markers • lined and unlined writing paper

Children illustrate a group-written story, and their drawings are bound together in a book. See page T101 for this week's Writing Center activity.

## Dramatic Play Center

> **Materials** • wagons, toys • blocks • toy cars

Children create a train to use in re-enacting *The Little Engine That Could*. Later they make a garage and take turns driving small cars in for "repairs." See pages T63 and T79 for this week's Dramatic Play Center activities.

## Science Center

> **Materials** • sheet of cardboard • toy cars • blocks • yardstick

Children experiment with releasing a toy car down a cardboard ramp. They change the slope and see how far the car travels each time. For a challenge, have children measure record the information, and report to the class. See page T73 for this week's Science Center activity.

## Math Center

> **Materials** • *Wheels Around* • counters • self-stick notes

Children look at the pictures of vehicles in the book and use counters to figure out the number of wheels on each one. See page T89 for this week's Math Center activity.

# Learning to Read
# Day 1

## Day at a Glance

### Learning to Read

**Read Aloud:**

***The Little Engine That Could***

☑ **Learning About / z /,** *page T66*

### Word Work

**High-Frequency Word Practice,** *page T68*

### Writing & Language

**Oral Language,** *page T69*

---

 **Half-Day Kindergarten**

☑ Indicates lessons for tested skills. Choose additional activities as time allows.

---

## Calendar

| Sunday | Monday | Tuesday | Wednesday | Thursday | Friday | Saturday |
|--------|--------|---------|-----------|----------|--------|----------|
|        |        |         | 1         | 2        | 3      | 4        |
| 5      | 6      | 7       | 8         | 9        | 10     | 11       |
| 12     | 13     | 14      | 15        | 16       | 17     | 18       |
| 19     | 20     | 21      | 22        | 23       | 24     | 25       |
| 26     | 27     | 28      | 29        | 30       | 31     |          |

To tie the calendar routine into the theme, have children suggest vehicle-shaped labels to mark the weather. For example, use a snowplow outline for a snowy day or a windshield with wipers for rainy weather.

## Daily Message

**Modeled Writing** Incorporate high-frequency words into the daily message. Call on volunteers to spell these words for you as you write.

> Miss Rossi is here for music class. We want to sing "The Wheels on the Bus."

Have children chant the spelling of each word on the wall today: **f-o-r** *spells* **for**; **s-e-e** *spells* **see**; **m-y** *spells* **my**.

## Daily Phonemic Awareness
### Blending Phonemes

- Read "To Market, To Market" on page 31 of *Higglety Pigglety.*

- Remind children that words are made up of small sounds. *I'll say some sounds. You put them together to make words from the poem:* /p//ĭ//g/ (pig); /h//ŏ//g/ (hog); /h//ō//m/ (home).

- Continue the game with other words with two or three sounds. For children who need help, try using familiar names: /m//ī//k/ (Mike).

**TO MARKET, TO MARKET**

To market, to market, to buy a fat pig,
Home again, home again, jiggety jig.
To market, to market, to buy a fat hog,
Home again, home again, jiggety jog.
To market, to market, to buy
a plum bun,
Home again, home again,
market is done.

**a Mother Goose Rhyme**

31

*Higglety Pigglety: A Book of Rhymes,* page 31

## Getting Ready to Learn

**To help plan their day, tell children that they will**

- listen to a story called *The Little Engine That Could.*

- meet a new Alphafriend, Zelda Zebra.

- act out a story in the Dramatic Play Center.

# Day 1

**Read Aloud**

**Purposes** • oral language • listening strategy • comprehension skill

### Selection Summary
This classic tale tells of a little engine who believed in herself and succeeded in doing a big job.

### Key Concepts
Trains, types of engines
Trying hard

# Teacher Read Aloud
## Oral Language/Comprehension

▶ **Building Background**

Display Teacher's Edition page T64. Read aloud the title and the author's name and the illustrators' names. Ask children who have seen or ridden on a train before to tell about it. *Where on a train can you find the engine? What is the engine's job?* (to pull the train) Have children tell how trains are similar to and different from some of the vehicles in *Wheels Around*.

### Strategy: Monitor/Clarify

**Teacher Modeling** Explain that sometimes readers or listeners come to something they don't understand in a story. Model the Monitor/Clarify Strategy.

**Think Aloud**

• *So far I've read the title,* The Little Engine That Could. *I'm a little confused: What is it that the Little Engine could do?*

• *What I should do is read on and look at the picture to see if my question is answered. As I read, listen and see if you can find out what the engine could do.*

### ✓ Comprehension Focus: Cause and Effect

**Teacher Modeling** Model how to identify cause-effect relationships.

**Think Aloud**

*Sometimes in a story, one thing happens and causes something else to happen. As I read, I'll think about what happens and what causes it. You think about why things happen, too.*

## ▶ Listening to the Story

Read the story dramatically to help give life to all the characters. Use a rhythmic cadence to read the "I can not," "I think I can," and "I thought I could," refrains to emulate the sound of a train's engine. You might have children chant with you.

Note that the Read Aloud art is also available on the back of the Theme Poster.

## ▶ Responding

**Summarizing the Story** Duplicate and cut out the pictures on **Blackline Masters 104–105** and attach felt to the back of each one. With yarn, outline a "mountain" on a flannelboard. As children summarize the story, add the pictures to the scene.

- *Who was on the little train? Where were they going?*

- *What kind of help did the little train need? Who did the dolls and toys on the train ask for help?*

- *Which engine was your favorite? Why?*

**Practice Book pages 203–204** Children complete the pages at small group time.

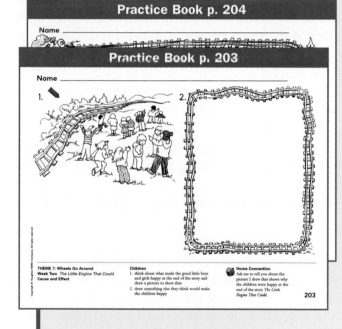

Practice Book p. 204

Practice Book p. 203

At Group Time

### Dramatic Play Center

Place a wagon loaded with toys in the Center. Children can then re-enact the story, making up conversations between the little train with the "load of toys" and the other engines.

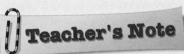
### Teacher's Note

Children enjoy stories in which hard work and determination pay off. Share other titles with children such as *Mike Mulligan and His Steam Shovel* by Virginia Lee Burton, *Little Toot* by Hardie Gramatky, or a version of *The Little Red Hen*.

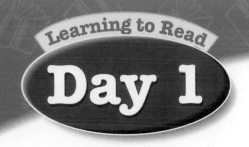
## The Little Engine That Could

Retold by Watty Piper

Illustration by George and Doris Hauman

Chug, chug, chug. Puff, puff, puff. Ding-dong, ding-dong. The little train rumbled over tracks.

She was a happy little train for she had such a jolly load to carry. Her cars were filled full of good things for boys and girls.

There were toy animals — giraffes with long necks, Teddy bears with almost no necks at all, and even a baby elephant. Then there were dolls — dolls with blue eyes and yellow curls, dolls with brown eyes and brown bobbed heads, and the funniest little toy clown you ever saw.

And there were cars full of toy engines, airplanes, tops, jack-knives, picture puzzles, books, and every kind of thing boys or girls could want.

But that was not all. Some of the cars were filled with all sorts of good things for boys and girls to eat — big golden oranges, red-cheeked apples, bottles of creamy milk for their breakfasts, fresh spinach for their dinners, peppermint drops, and lollipops for after-meal treats. The little train was carrying all these wonderful things to the good little boys and girls on the other side of the mountain.

She puffed along merrily. Then all of a sudden she stopped with a jerk. She simply could not go another inch. She tried and she tried, but her wheels would not turn. **(Ask:** *Why do you think the little train couldn't go another inch?***)**

What were all those good little boys and girls on the other side of the mountain going to do without the wonderful toys to play with and the good food to eat?

"Here comes a shiny new engine," said the funny little clown who jumped out of the train.

"Let us ask him to help us."

So all the dolls and toys cried out together, "Please, Shiny New Engine, won't you please pull our train over the mountain? Our engine has broken down, and the boys and girls on the other side won't have any toys to play with or good food to eat unless you help us." **(Say:** *The dolls have flagged down another train. What happened in this story that made them do that? Do you think the Shiny New Engine will help?***)**

But the Shiny New Engine snorted: "I pull you? I am a Passenger Engine. I have just carried a fine big train over the mountain, with more cars than you ever dreamed of. My train had sleeping cars, with comfortable berths; a dining car where waiters bring whatever hungry people want to eat; and parlor cars in which people sit in soft armchairs and look out of big plate-glass windows. I pull the likes of you? Indeed not!"

And off he steamed to the roundhouse, where engines live when they are not busy. How sad the little train and all the dolls and toys felt!

Then the little clown called out, "The Passenger Engine is not the only one in the world. Here is another engine coming, a great big strong one. Let us ask him to help us."

The little toy clown waved his flag and the big strong engine came to a stop.

"Please, oh, please, Big Engine," cried all the dolls and toys together. "Won't you please pull our train over the mountain? Our engine has broken down, and the good little boys and girls on the other side won't have any toys to play with or good food to eat unless you help us."

But the Big Strong Engine bellowed: "I am a Freight Engine. I have just pulled a big train loaded with big machines over the mountain. These machines print books and newspapers for grown-ups to read. I am a very important engine indeed. I won't pull the likes of you!" And the Freight Engine puffed off indignantly to the roundhouse. **(Say:** *Let's name the engines that would not help so far: The Shiny New Passenger Engine and the Big Strong Freight Engine. Why do you think they wouldn't help?***)**

The little train and all the dolls and toys were very sad.

"Cheer up," cried the little toy clown. "The Freight Engine is not the only one in the world. Here comes another. He looks very old and tired, but our train is so little, perhaps he can help us."

So the little toy clown waved his flag and the dingy, rusty old engine stopped.

"Please, Kind Engine," cried all the dolls and toys together. "Won't you please pull our train over the mountain? Our engine has broken down, and the boys and girls on the other side won't have any toys to play with or good food to eat unless you help us."

But the Rusty Old Engine sighed, "I am so tired. I must rest my weary wheels. I cannot pull even so little a train as yours over the mountain. I can not. I can not. I can not."

And off he rumbled to the roadhouse chugging, "I can not. I can not. I can not."

**(Ask:** *Who remembers the story title? Have we met the little engine in the title yet? Let's read on to find out what kind of engine it is.***)**

Then indeed the little train was very, very sad, and the dolls and toys were ready to cry. But the little clown called out, "Here is another engine coming, a little blue engine, a very little one, maybe she will help us."

The very little engine came chug, chugging merrily along. When she saw the toy clown's flag, she stopped quickly.

"What's the matter, my friends?" she asked kindly.

"Oh, Little Blue Engine," cried the dolls and toys. "Will you pull us over the mountain? Our engine has broken down, and the good boys and girls on the other side won't have any toys to play with or good food to eat, unless you help us. Please, please help us, Little Blue Engine."

"I'm not very big," said the Little Blue Engine. "They use me only for switching trains in the yard. I have never been over the mountain."

"But we must get over the mountain before the children awake," said all the dolls and the toys.

The very little engine looked up and saw the tears in the dolls' eyes. And she thought of the good little boys and girls on the other side of the mountain who would not have any toys or good food unless she helped.

Then she said, "I think I can. I think I can. I think I can." And she hitched herself to the little train. **(Ask:** *How is what the Little Blue Engine said different from what the Rusty Old Engine said? Do you think she can? Let's listen and find out.***)**

She tugged and pulled and pulled and tugged and slowly, slowly, slowly they started off. The toy clown jumped aboard and all the dolls and the animals began to smile and cheer.

Puff, puff, chug, chug, went the Little Blue Engine. "I think I can — I think I can — I think I can — I think I can — I think I can — I think I can — I think I can — I think I can."

Up, up, up. Faster and faster and faster the little engine climbed, until at last they reached the top of the mountain.

Down in the valley lay the city.

"Hurray, hurray, " cried the funny little clown and all the dolls and toys. "The good little boys and girls in the city will be happy because you helped us, Kind Little Blue Engine."

And the Little Blue Engine smiled and seemed to say as she puffed steadily down the mountain...

"I thought I could. I thought I could. I thought I could. I thought I could. I thought I could. I thought I could. **(Ask:** *Why do you think the Little Blue Engine was able to do such a hard job?***)**

# Learning to Read
# Day 1

## OBJECTIVES

**Children**

- identify pictures whose names begin with /z/

## MATERIALS

- **Alphafriend Cards** *Larry Lion, Pippa Pig, Zelda Zebra*
- **Alphafriend Audiotape** Theme 7
- **Alphafolder** *Zelda Zebra*
- **Picture Cards** for *z, p,* and *l*
- **Phonics Center:** Theme 7, Week 2, Day 1

### Home Connection

A take-home version of Zelda Zebra's song is on an **Alphafriends Blackline Master.** Children can share the song with their families.

### English Language Learners

Check to make sure children are voicing /z/. As needed, have them place their fingers against their throats to feel the vibration. Ask children to exaggerate the buzzing sound of /z/ to ensure contrast with /s/.

# Phonemic Awareness
## ✓ Beginning Sound

▶ **Introducing the Alphafriend: Zelda Zebra**

Use the Alphafriend routine to introduce Zelda Zebra.

**1 Alphafriend Riddle** Read these clues:

- *This Alphafriend is an animal. Her sound is /z/. Say it with me: /z/.*
- *You might see this Alphafriend in a zzzoo.*
- *She looks like a horse with black and white stripes.*

When most hands are up, call on children until they guess *zebra.*

**2 Pocket Chart** Display Zelda Zebra in a pocket chart. Say her name, stretching the /z/ sound slightly. Have children echo you.

**3** 📼 **Alphafriend Audiotape** Play Zelda Zebra's song. *Listen for words that start with /z/.*

**4 Alphafolder** Children name the /z/ pictures in the illustration.

**5 Summarize**

- *What is our Alphafriend's name? What is her sound?*
- *What words in our Alphafriend's song start with /z/?*
- *Each time you look at Zelda Zebra this week, remember the /z/ sound.*

### Zelda Zebra's Song
**(Tune: "L'il Liza Jane")**

Zelda Zebra likes to zoom.
 She zooms with zest.
Zelda Zebra zig zags too.
 She does her best.
Zelda Zebra makes one big Z.
Zelda Zebra zips right past me!

## ► Listening for / z /

**Compare and Review: / p /, / l /** Display Alphafriends *Pippa Pig* and *Larry Lion* opposite *Zelda Zebra*. Review each character's sound.

Hold up the Picture Cards one at a time. Children signal "thumbs up" for pictures that start with Zelda Zebra's sound, / z /, and a volunteer puts the card below Zelda's picture. For "thumbs down" words, volunteers put cards below the correct Alphafriends.

Pictures: *zipper, peach, leaf, purse, zip, lemon, zigzag, log, pot*

Tell children that they will sort more pictures today in the Phonics Center.

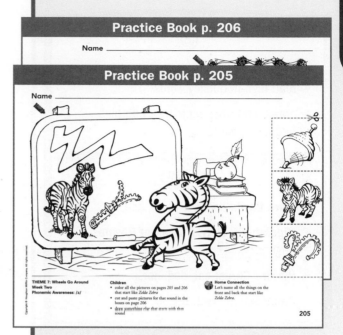

Practice Book p. 206

Name _____

Practice Book p. 205

Name _____

## ► Apply

**Practice Book pages 205–206** Children will complete the pages at small group time.

### At Group Time

## Phonics Center

Use the Phonics Center materials for **Theme 7, Week 2, Day 1**.

**Phonemic Awareness** (T67)

# Day 1

## OBJECTIVES

**Children**

- read high-frequency words
- create and write sentences with high-frequency words

## MATERIALS

- **Word Cards** *and, I, like, my, see, to*
- *Higglety Pigglety: A Book of Rhymes,* page 32
- **Picture Cards:** cat, dog, horse
- **Punctuation Card:** period

# High-Frequency Word Practice

▶ **Matching Words**

- Display Word Cards for *see, and, like, to, I, my* in a pocket chart. Call on children to identify each word and to match it on the Word Wall. Remind children that they will see these words often in books.

- Hold up Word cards *to* and *see.* *I'll read a poem. You listen for these two words.*

- Read "Hey, Diddle, Diddle." *Did you hear these words in the poem?* Track the print as you reread the line with those words. *Who will match the cards to the same words in this line?*

- Repeat with *and.*

**Higglety Pigglety: A Book of Rhymes, page 32**

**Writing Opportunity** Add Picture Cards for *dog, cat,* and *horse* to the pocket chart. Begin a sentence with *I like,* and have volunteers add cards to complete it. Then encourage children to make up their own sentences to write. They can refer to the cards, use their knowledge of letter sounds to spell other words, and add drawings. Provide time for children to share their work.

# Oral Language

## ▶ Using Position Words

*In* **The Little Engine That Could** *where were the dolls, toys, and food?* (on a train) ***Where were the cars holding the dolls, toys, and food?*** (behind the engine, on the tracks) Explain that words like *on* and *behind* tell where things are.

**Viewing** Use the prompts below to help children brainstorm a list of position words. List the words on a chart.

- ■ *Where am I standing?* (beside the chart, in front of the group) *Where is Janna sitting?* (next to Gary, behind Wendy, on the floor)

- ■ Move your marker to different places in the room, and have children tell where it is: under a chair, in the box, over the table.

- ■ Review the chart, adding simple line drawings to help children "read" it.

### At Group Time
# Writing Center

Put the chart in the Writing Center. Partners can review the pictures and talk about position words. Then have each child draw one favorite thing from *The Little Engine That Could* and write or dictate a label to describe its position.

behind

### OBJECTIVES
⊙

**Children**
- • use position words

### MATERIALS

- • **Read Aloud:** *The Little Engine That Could*

---

**MEETING INDIVIDUAL NEEDS**

### English Language Learners

Choice of prepositions varies a great deal among languages. Expect interference from children's first language. Provide practice by placing items in various positions in relation to each other. Ask: Where's the _____? As children answer, assist them with vocabulary and usage as needed.

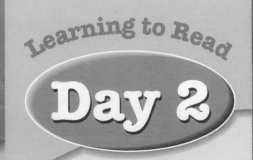

## Learning to Read
# Day 2

## Day at a Glance

### Learning to Read

**Big Book:**

*Vroom, Chugga, Vroom-Vroom*

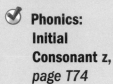 **Phonics:** Initial Consonant z, *page T74*

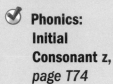 **High-Frequency Word: have,** *page T76*

### Word Work

**High-Frequency Word Practice,** *page T78*

### Writing & Language

**Vocabulary Expansion,** *page T79*

---

 **Half-Day Kindergarten**

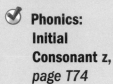 Indicates lessons for tested skills. Choose additional activities as time allows.

---

# Opening

## Calendar

| | | | | | | |
|---|---|---|---|---|---|---|
| Sunday | Monday | Tuesday | Wednesday | Thursday | Friday | Saturday |
| | | | 1 | 2 | 3 | 4 |
| 5 | 6 | 7 | 8 | 9 | 10 | 11 |
| 12 | 13 | 14 | 15 | 16 | 17 | 18 |
| 19 | 20 | 21 | 22 | 23 | 24 | 25 |
| 26 | 27 | 28 | 29 | 30 | 31 | |

first ... last

Extend yesterday's discussion of position words to your calendar routine. *Who will show us the name of the day that is first every week? Which day is last? What is today's date? What number do you see before (after) it?*

## Daily Message

**Modeled Writing** As you write today's news, pause to point out any words that tell where (position words). Have children tell why those words are helpful.

Today Marita will put food <u>in</u> Hammie's cage.

Mark will put olive oil <u>on</u> Hammie's wheel.

### Word Wall

Have partners read and spell words on the wall today. Each partner can name five words for the other child to find and spell.

## Daily Phonemic Awareness
### Blending Phonemes

- Read "Zebra" on page 33 of *Higglety Pigglety*.

- Play a guessing game. *I'll say some sounds. You put them together to make color words from the poem: / wh / / ī / / t /.* (white) *Now here's a hard one, with four sounds. Listen: / b / / l / / ă / / k /.* (black)

- Continue the game with other words with two or three sounds: *red, zoo, zip, see.*

**ZEBRA**

Zebra.
Zebra.
Which is right —

White on black —
Or black on white?

by Langston Hughes

33

***Higglety Pigglety: A Book of Rhymes, page 33***

## Getting Ready to Learn

**To help plan their day, tell children that they will**

- listen to a Big Book: *Vroom, Chugga, Vroom-Vroom.*

- learn the new letters *Z* and *z*, and look for words that begin with *z*.

- compare how far toy cars travel on a ramp in the Science Center.

### Big Book

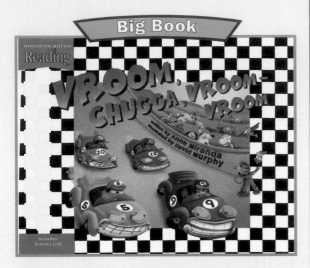

**Purposes** • concepts of print • story language
• reading strategy • comprehension skill

**Selection Summary**
Fast-paced, rhyming text describes the adventures of animal characters who compete in a great auto race.

**Key Concepts**
Races and contests
Parts of a car

# Sharing the Big Book
## Oral Language/Comprehension

▶ **Building Background**

Share the Big Book's title and by-line. Then take a picture walk. Explain that the story is make-believe but that it shows many things found in real car races. Ask children who have seen a real car race on TV to tell how it was like the one pictured. Discuss how the helmets, the numerals on the cars, and the starting flag are used.

### Strategy: Monitor/Clarify

**Teacher Modeling** Model how to clarify anything confusing in a story.

**Think Aloud**

*If I've never been to a real car race, I may read things I don't understand. If I am confused by something, I can go back and read again. I can also look at the pictures for help. If I am still confused, I can ask someone to explain that part.*

### ✓ Comprehension Focus: Cause and Effect

**Teacher Modeling** Remind children that if they think about why things happen in a story, they will understand it better and enjoy it more.

**Think Aloud**

*Sometimes one thing happens and causes something else to happen. On the cover I see the crowd cheering and small clouds coming from the cars. I think the artist wanted me to figure out that the cars were going really fast. That's what caused those other things. As we read, let's think about why things happen.*

## ▶ Sharing the Story

Read the selection, emphasizing the rhyme. Pause occasionally to let children contribute car numbers or rhyming words.

## ▶ Responding

**Personal Response** Encourage children to use the language of the story as they react to it.

- *What did you like best about the story?*

- *What did you learn about cars that you didn't know before? about car races?*

- *What was your favorite car in the race? Why?*

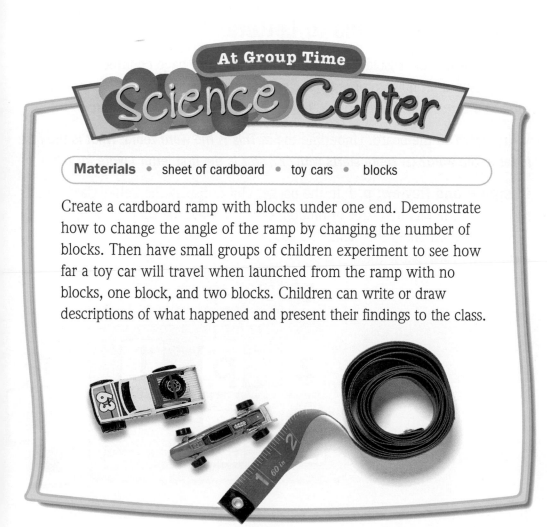

**At Group Time**

### Science Center

Materials • sheet of cardboard • toy cars • blocks

Create a cardboard ramp with blocks under one end. Demonstrate how to change the angle of the ramp by changing the number of blocks. Then have small groups of children experiment to see how far a toy car will travel when launched from the ramp with no blocks, one block, and two blocks. Children can write or draw descriptions of what happened and present their findings to the class.

**MEETING INDIVIDUAL NEEDS**

**Extra Support**

Reinforce position words by pointing to various cars in the story and having a child describe where they are.

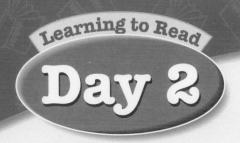
## OBJECTIVES

**Children**

- identify words that begin with /z/
- identify pictures whose names begin with the letter z
- form the letters Z, z

## MATERIALS

- **Alphafriend Card** *Zelda Zebra*
- **Letter Cards** *l, p, z*
- **Picture Cards** for *z, p,* and *l*
- **Blackline Master 182**
- **Phonics Center:** Theme 7, Week 2, Day 2

**Extra Support**

To help children remember the sound for z, point out that the letter's name gives a clue to its sound: z, /z/.

# Phonics

## ✓ Initial Consonant z

### ▶ Develop Phonemic Awareness

**Beginning Sound** Read aloud the lyrics to Zelda Zebra's song and have children echo it line-for-line. Have them listen for the /z/ words and signal "thumbs up" for each one they hear.

> **Zelda Zebra's Song**
> (Tune: "L'il Liza Jane")
>
> Zelda Zebra likes to zoom.
>   She zooms with zest.
> Zelda Zebra zig zags too.
>   She does her best.
> Zelda Zebra makes one big Z.
> Zelda Zebra zips right past me!

### ▶ Connect Sounds to Letters

**Beginning Letter** Display the *Zelda Zebra* card, and have children name the letter pictured on her. Say: *The letter z stands for the sound /z/, as in zebra. When you see a z, remember Zelda Zebra. That will help you remember the sound /z/.*

Write *zebra* on the board. Underline the *z*. *This is the word* zebra. *What is the first letter in the word?* (z) *Zebra starts with /z/, so z is the first letter I write for* zebra.

**Compare and Review: *p, l*** In the pocket chart, display the Letter Cards as shown and the Picture Cards in random order. Review the sounds for *z, p,* and *l*. Have children take turns naming a picture, saying its beginning sound, and putting the card below the right letter.

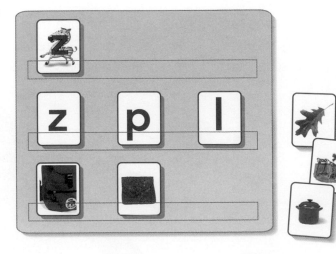

Tell children that they will sort more pictures in the Phonics Center today.

## ▶ Handwriting

**Writing Z, z** Tell children that now they'll learn to write the letters that stand for / z /: capital *Z* and small *z*. Write each letter as you recite the hand-writing rhyme. Children can chant each rhyme as they "write" the letter in the air.

### Handwriting Rhyme: Z

From the top, zip right with a line.
Slant down
to the left, and zip right one more time:
It's a Z, big Z, big Z!

### Handwriting Rhyme: z

From the middle, zip right with a line.
Slant down to the left, and zip right one more time:
It's a z, a small z, small z!

## ▶ Apply

**Practice Book page 207** Children will complete the page at small group time.

**Blackline Master 182** This page provides additional handwriting practice for small group time.

### At Group Time
# Phonics Center

Use Phonics Center materials for **Theme 7, Week 2, Day 2**.

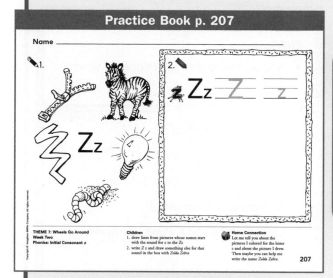

### Practice Book p. 207

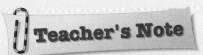

## 📎 Teacher's Note

Handwriting practice for the continuous stroke style is available on **Blackline Master 208**.

### 🗄 Portfolio Opportunity

Save the **Practice Book** page to show children's grasp of the letter-sound association.
Save the **Blackline Master 182** for a handwriting sample.

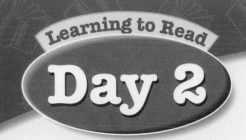
## OBJECTIVES

**Children**

• read and write the high-frequency word *have*

## MATERIALS

• **Word Cards** *A, a, have, I*
• **Picture Cards** *dog, farm, feet, pig*
• **Punctuation Card:** period
• *Higglety Pigglety: A Book of Rhymes,* page 20

### Teacher's Note

You will need to prepare cards for *big, can,* and *2* for this lesson.

# ☑ High-Frequency Word

## *New Word:* have

### ▶ Teach

Tell children that today they will learn to read and write a word that they will often see in stories. Say *have* and use it in context.

I *have* a bike.    I *have* to go home.    I *have* two dolls.

Invite children to use the word *have* in oral sentences. Then write *have* on the board, and ask children to spell it as you point to the letters. Say: **Spell have with me, h-a-v-e, have.** Lead a chant, clapping on each beat, to help children remember the spelling: **h-a-v-e, have! h-a-v-e, have!**

**Word Wall** Post *have* on the Word Wall, and remind children to look there when they need to remember how to write the word.

### ▶ Practice

**Reading** Make cards for *big, can* and the numeral 2. Then build the sentences shown in the pocket chart. Children take turns reading aloud. Place the pocket chart in the Phonics Center so that children can practice building and reading sentences on their own.

Display page 20 of *Higglety Pigglety*.

- Share the rhyme "Notice."

- Reread the poem, tracking the print and asking children to listen for the word *have*. Then recite the first line and ask a child to point to *have*.

**Notice**

I have a dog,
I had a cat.
I've got a frog
Inside my hat.

by David McCord

20

*Higglety Pigglety: A Book of Rhymes*, page 20

. . . . . . . . . . . . . . . . . . . . . . . . . . . . . . . . . . . . . . . . . . . . . . . . . . . . . . . . . . . . .

▶ **Apply**

**Practice Book page 208** Children will read and write *have* as they complete the Practice Book page. On Day 3, they will practice reading *have* in the **Phonics Library** story "Tan Van."

**Practice Book p. 208**

Name _____

✏ [ have ] _____

_____

I _____ to sit here.    I _____ a pan.

I _____ to hit it.    I _____ a cat.

THEME 7: Wheels Go Around
Week Two
High-Frequency Word *have*

**Children**
• practice writing *have* on the lines at the top
• read the sentences above the boxes and write *have* to complete them
• choose and circle one sentence for each box
• draw a picture to go with it

**Home Connection**
Let me read these sentences to you! I drew pictures to go with two of the sentences. Let me tell you about them.

208

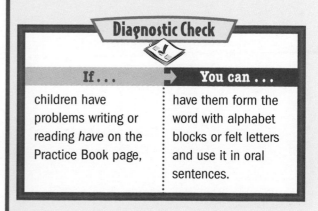

**Diagnostic Check**

| If... | You can... |
|---|---|
| children have problems writing or reading *have* on the Practice Book page, | have them form the word with alphabet blocks or felt letters and use it in oral sentences. |

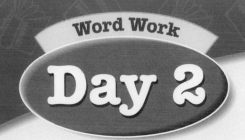

# Day 2

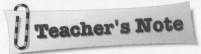

## Teacher's Note

You will need to create the word cards *big* and *can* for this lesson.

# High-Frequency Word Practice

## ▶ Building Sentences

Tell children that you want to build a sentence about things with wheels.

■ Display the Word Cards and Picture Cards in random order. Put the Word Card *I* in the pocket chart and read it.

■ *I want the next word to be* have. *Who can find that word? That's right! This word is* have. *Now who can read my sentence so far?*

■ Continue building the sentence *I have a big _____*. Children choose a picture to complete it.

■ Read the sentence together. Then continue with a new one.

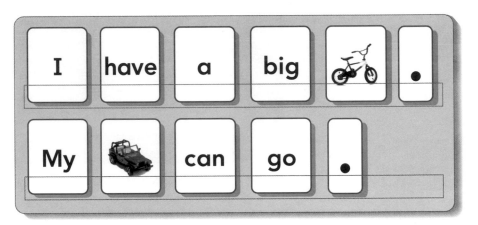

**Writing Opportunity** Have each child write a sentence, using one from the pocket chart as a model. Children can choose a vehicle and add their own drawings. If children choose to write a different sentence, remind them to use what they know about letter sounds to help them spell the words.

I have a new blue bike.

# Vocabulary Expansion

## ▶ Position Words, Parts of a Car

**Viewing and Speaking** Briefly review yesterday's work with words that tell where. Then page through *Vroom, Chugga, Vroom-Vroom* together and ask children to describe where some of the cars are in each scene.

- Explain that position words can also tell where parts of a car are.

- Duplicate the car on **Blackline Master 106** and tape it to the center of a sheet of chart paper. Point to parts of the car and help children name them; add a label for each part.

- Duplicate and cut out the pictures of the auto parts on **Blackline Master 107**. Children can match them to the same parts on the diagram and use position words to tell where each part of the car is. For example, children might say a handle is *on* the door or a windshield is *behind* the hood.

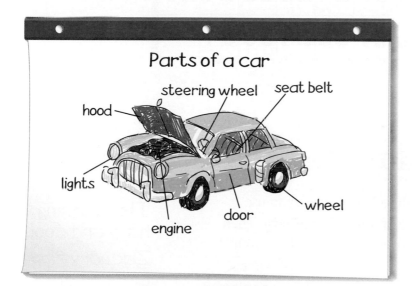

Parts of a car

steering wheel    seat belt
hood
lights
engine    door    wheel

## At Group Time
## Dramatic Play Center

**Materials** • blocks • toy cars and trucks

Have groups of children use blocks to outline "bays" in a "garage." Children can take turns "driving" small toy cars pulling into the garage, working on them, and backing them out. Encourage conversations about the cars' positions and features.

MEETING INDIVIDUAL NEEDS

**English Language Learners**

Most English language learners will not know the parts of a car. Encourage these children to repeat the words English speakers name. Check for correct pronunciation of all the vowel sounds.

# Day 3

# Opening

## Day at a Glance

### Learning to Read

**Big Book:**

*Vroom, Chugga, Vroom-Vroom*

☑ **Phonics:**
*Blending z
-ig, page T90*

### Word Work

**Building Words,** *page T92*

### Writing & Language

**Shared Writing,** *page T93*

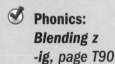

---

**Half-Day Kindergarten**

☑ Indicates lessons for tested skills. Choose additional activities as time allows.

---

## Calendar

| Sunday | Monday | Tuesday | Wednesday | Thursday | Friday | Saturday |
|--------|--------|---------|-----------|----------|--------|----------|
|        |        |         | 1         | 2        | 3      | 4        |
| 5      | 6      | 7       | 8         | 9        | 10     | 11       |
| 12     | 13     | 14      | 15        | 16       | 17     | 18       |
| 19     | 20     | 21      | 22        | 23       | 24     | 25       |
| 26     | 27     | 28      | 29        | 30       | 31     |          |

To add variety to your calendar routine, suggest a "race" between sunny, cloudy, rainy, and snowy days. For the remainder of the month, children can write each day's date and draw a weather symbol. At month's end they can see which weather "wins."

## Daily Message

**Modeled Writing** Try to use *z* words in the daily message. Then call on volunteers to circle each *z*. Help children see that letters stand for sounds in the beginning, the middle, and the end of a word.

> This morning was
> ha(z)y and cool.
> (Z)achary (z)ipped
> up his coat.
> Katie wore a fu(zz)y
> sweater.

Choose a child to point to and read the new word that was added to the wall this week, *have*. Children can compare *have* to other words on the wall. *(Have has four letters like here and like; begins with / h / like here; ends with an e like see, here.)*

## Daily Phonemic Awareness
### Blending Phonemes

Tell children that you will say some sounds and they should put them together to make a word that names part of a car.

- Pronounce /s/ /ē/ /t/, have children repeat the sounds with you, and then have someone say the word. (seat)

- Continue with these sounds: /h/ /ō̄o/ /d/ (hood); /wh/ /ē/ /l/ (wheel); /l/ /ī/ /t/ (light).

- Now use the same words to play "Pat, Pat, Clap."

## Getting Ready to Learn

**To help plan their day, tell children that they will**

- reread and talk about the Big Book *Vroom, Chugga, Vroom-Vroom.*

- read a story called "Tan Van."

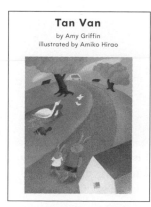

- read, write, and explore more about wheels in the Centers.

DAY 3

# Sharing the Big Book

**Big Book**

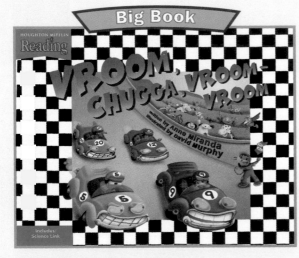

**Reading for Understanding** Reread the story, emphasizing the rhythm and rhyme. Pause for discussion points.

**Oral Language**

On a rereading, point out the words that name or mimic sounds:

**vroom, chugga, vroom-vroom** the sound of the racing cars' engines

**boom** the sound of hearts pounding

**zoom** the sound of speed

Vroom, chugga, vroom-vroom.
Race is going to start soon!

**page 1**

Banners wave.
Fans cheer!

Cars are checked.
The start's near.

**pages 2–3**

1 is at the starting gate.
2 and 3 can hardly wait.

4 and 5 check brakes and lights.
6 makes sure his seatbelt's tight.

**pages 4–5**

7's in the pole position.
8 and 9 start their ignitions.

10 and 11 zip up suits.
12 and 13 put on boots.

6                                    7

**pages 6–7**

14, 15 call their crews.
16 tightens two loose screws.

17, 18 rev in place.
19 wants to set the pace.

8                                    9

**pages 8–9**

20 lines up last in row.
Green lights flash.
Get ready, GO!

Vroom, chugga, VROOM-VROOM!
Hearts pound, BOOM, BOOM!
Flag waves and ZOOM, ZOOM!

10                                   11

**pages 10–11**

## ▶ Supporting Comprehension

title page

### ✓ Comprehension Focus: Cause and Effect

**Teacher-Student Modeling** Review that good readers think about what happens in a story and *why*. Prompts:

- *The animals are hurrying. Can you tell why?* (The race will start soon.)

pages 6–7

### Strategy: Monitor/Clarify

**Teacher-Student Modeling** Remind children that if they do not understand something, the pictures can help. Prompts:

- *How does the picture help explain what "start their ignitions" means?* (Exhaust shows the cars are running; the ignition must start a car's engine.)

**DAY 3**

pages 8–9

### Drawing Conclusions

- *Why do 14 and 15 call their crews?* (14 has a flat; 15 is sick.) *What does a crew do?* (take care of cars)

**Revisiting the Text**

pages 10–11

## Concepts of Print

### ✓ Matching words; Using all capitals

- Frame *go* on page 10 and have children spell it; do the same with *go* on the Word Wall. *A word is always spelled the same.*

- *Words spelled with all capital letters show excitement.* Frame *Go* in the art on 10 and 11; have children spell it and then say it as the starter would.

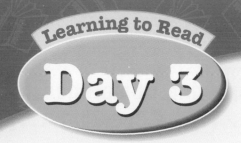
▶ ## Supporting Comprehension

**pages 12–13**

**Drawing Conclusions**

■ *What is made of rubber on a car?* (tire, wheels)
*How does the picture show that the tires are burning, or losing rubber?* (by the marks on the road)

**pages 14–15**

**Noting Details**

■ *What job do you think the bird on page 14 has? How do you know that?* (race announcer; has a microphone)

**pages 16–17**

### Strategy: Monitor/Clarify

**Teacher-Student Modeling** *What does it mean to blow a tire? How does the picture show this? ... What is the pit?* (an area off the track where cars are fixed) *What could you do if the picture and rereading didn't help you understand what a pit is?* (ask someone for help)

**Teacher's Note**

**Language Patterns** On a rereading, point out how the author compares things to describe them: *hearts pound* (like a hammer); *down the straight they* (the cars) *flash like lightning.*

Rubber, rubber, burn, burn . . .

12

Racers take the first turn.

13

**pages 12–13**

Down the straight they flash like lightning. Hold your breath. It's so exciting!

14

Speeding madly 'round the curve, Number 3 begins to swerve.

15

**pages 14–15**

16's blown his left rear tire. 7's engine has caught on fire!

16

12 and 13 have to quit. 17 is in the pit.

17

**pages 16–17**

19 just ran out of gas.
11's blocked and cannot pass.

4 is stuck in second gear.
Number 6 brings up the rear.

18

19

**pages 18–19**

8 just made a big mistake.
18 has to hit the brake.

10 and 20 brush the wall.
15's muffler's going to fall.

20

21

**pages 20–21**

2 and 5 are nose to nose.
14's steering wheel just froze.

1 is spinning off the track.
Several cars are falling back.

22

23

**pages 22–23**

▶ **Supporting Comprehension**

pages 18–21

**Comprehension Focus:
Cause and Effect**

**Student Modeling** *What happens to car 11 (page 18)? Why can't it pass?* (It's blocked.) *What does car 18 do (page 20)? Why does it have to hit its breaks?* (to avoid hitting the bugs crossing the track)

page 22–23

**Making Judgments**

■ *Why do you think most of the cars in the story are having trouble?* (They are driving too fast.) *Away from the race track, real drivers have speed limits and other traffic rules to follow. Why?*

**DAY 3**

**Challenge**

Children who can easily match words in the text may be able to find and read words from the Word Wall or familiar families. At small group time, give these children a list of things to find in the story.

**Sharing the Big Book** **T85**

## Learning to Read
# Day 3

▶ ## Supporting Comprehension

**pages 24–25**

**Making Inferences**

■ *Which car is ahead on page 24? Which car do you think will win the race?* (number 9) *What does a car have to do to win a race?* (cross the finish line)

**page 26**

**Characters**

■ *How do you think the driver feels about winning the race? How do you know?*

**page 27**

**Making Inferences**

■ *What do you think will happen next? Why?*
(Another race will start; cars are lining up.)

- - - - - - - - - - - - - - - - - - - - - - - - - - - -
**page 29**

## Strategy: Monitor/Clarify

**Student Modeling** *What can you do to figure out what the word test means here?*
(look at the picture, read on) *What does test mean in this story?* (a contest, a race)
- - - - - - - - - - - - - - - - - - - - - - - - - - - -

**English Language Learners**

Revisit the text with a small group and let children tell you what is happening in each picture. After discussing each page, read the text to confirm or clarify children's explanations.

Vroom, chugga, vroom-vroom! Someone's going to win soon!

24

Which car's first across the line? Hurrah! It's driver number 9!

25

**pages 24–25**

9 has won a golden cup.

26

But look!  More cars are lining up.

27

**pages 26–27**

There's going to be another race.

28

Another test.  Another chase.

29

**pages  28–29**

Vroom, chugga, vroom-vroom.
Start your engine! ZOOM-ZOOM!

30

**page 30**

▶ **Supporting Comprehension**

page 30

**Making Judgments**

■ *How do the fans feel about the start of a new race? How does the driver feel? Do you think you would like to see a car race? Why or why not?*

 **Comprehension Focus: Cause and Effect**

**Student Modeling** Have children browse through the book to find examples of something that happened and what caused it. Children can tell in their own words what happened in the picture and why.

**DAY 3**

 **English Language Learners**

Tell children you will read the story again, pausing whenever they want you to talk about something. Encourage all children to raise their hands when they want to stop and hear more about what something means.

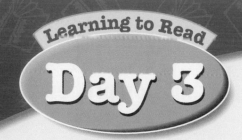

# Day 3

### Practice Book p. 209

Name _____

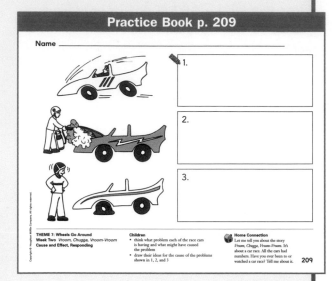

1.

2.

3.

THEME 7: Wheels Go Around
Week Two *Vroom, Chugga, Vroom-Vroom*
Cause and Effect, Responding

Children
• think what problem each of the race cars is having and what might have caused the problem
• draw their ideas for the cause of the problems shown in 1, 2, and 3

Home Connection
Let me tell you about the story *Vroom, Chugga, Vroom-Vroom*. It's about a car race. All the cars had numbers. Have you ever been to or watched a car race? Tell me about it.

209

> ## Responding to the Story

**Retelling** Use these prompts to help children summarize the story:

■ *Where does this story take place? What is it about?*

■ *What kinds of problems did some of the cars have? What caused the problems?*

■ *Which car won the race?*

■ *What did you like best about the story?*

**Literature Circle** Have small groups compare the cars in this story to real ones. *What parts of this story are like things in real life? What makes this story make-believe?*

**Practice Book page 209** Children will complete the page at small group time.

### Diagnostic Check

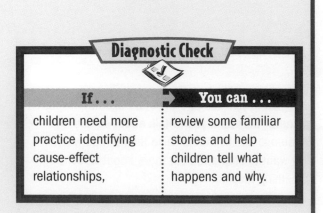

| If... | You can ... |
|-------|-------------|
| children need more practice identifying cause-effect relationships, | review some familiar stories and help children tell what happens and why. |

## At Group Time
# Art Center

**Materials** • construction paper rectangles, squares, circles • glue

Cut out rectangles, squares, and circles of various colors and sizes and place them in the Art Center. Children can arrange the shapes on paper to design cars, glue them in place, and add details with crayons or markers.

## At Group Time
# Math Center

**Materials** • *Wheels Around* • *Vroom, Chugga, Vroom-Vroom* • counters • self-stick notes

Introduce the activity by displaying a side-view picture of a car in either book. Point out that although only two wheels are shown, two more appear on the other side of the car.

Put down two counters for the two visible wheels, then two more for the ones that can't be seen. Don't forget to add one for the steering wheel! Count the markers, write 5 on the self-stick note, and post it at the edge of the page. At group time, children can follow your example to find out how many wheels the different vehicles in *Wheels Around* have.

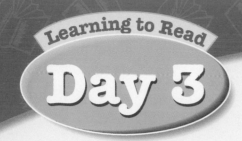
### Practice Book p. 210

Name _____

┌─────────────────┐
│  Zig   dig   pig │
└─────────────────┘

1. _____
   My _____ is Zig.
   ☺  ☹

2. _____
   Zig can _____ .
   ☺  ☹

3. _____
   Here is my pig _____ .
   ☺  ☹

THEME 7: Wheels Go Around
Week Two
Phonics: z, -ig

**Children**
- read the sentences and write words ending in -ig to complete them
- mark the smile (yes) or the frown (no) to show whether the picture goes with the sentence beside it.

**Home Connection**
Let me read these sentences to you! These will help me write the letters Z, i, d, p, and g on separate scraps of paper? We can build words with them.

210

# Phonics

## ✓ *Blending z -ig*

### ▶ Connect Sounds to Letters

**Review Consonant *z*** Play Zelda Zebra's song, and have children clap for each /z/ word. Write *Z* and *z* on the board, and list words from the song.

**Blending *-ig*** Recall that children can build words with consonant letters and a vowel ("helper letter"). Display Alphafriend *Iggy Iguana*.

*Iggy Iguana will help us build words today. Iggy's letter is the vowel* i, *and one sound* i *stands for is* /ĭ/. Hold up the Letter Card *i. Say* /ĭ/. *Listen for* /ĭ/ *in these words:* /ĭ/ if, /ĭ/ inch, /ĭ/ igloo.

Hold up the Letter Cards *d* and *g* and review their sounds. Stretch out the sounds in *dig*: /d//ĭ//g/. Build *dig* in the pocket chart and have children blend it with you, sound by sound.

**Blending *-ig* Words** Take away the *d* and hold up Letter Card *z*. Put *z* in front of *ig,* and model blending /z//ig/, *zig*. Tell children that *zig* means to move to the side quickly. Then have them blend the sounds in *zig* while you point. Model blending *-ig* with other consonants to make *big, fig, pig,* and *rig*.

**Word Wall** Point to *dig* on the Word Wall. Remind children that it will help them build words that rhyme with *dig*.

### ▶ Apply

**Practice Book page 210** Children complete the page at small group time.

Phonics in Action

Reading
Phonics Library

Wheels Go Around

# Applying Phonics Skills and High-Frequency Words

## ▶ Introducing the Story

Display the cover and discuss the illustration. Ask children what clues in the art tell them about the weather. Then do a brief picture walk and point out the cat and the pig.

### Phonics/Decoding Strategy

**Teacher-Student Modeling** Print *Zig Pig* on the board and explain that it is the name of one of the characters in the story. Discuss using the Phonics/Decoding Strategy to read the name.

**Think Aloud**

*The name begins with capital Z. The sound for Z is / z /. I know the sounds for i, g: / ĭ // g /, -ig. Let's blend: / z // ig /, Zig. Now who will show us how to figure out Zig's last name?*

## ▶ Coached Reading

Have children read each page silently before reading with you. Prompts:

**page 1** Model how to blend *Tan*, the first word in the title. Have volunteers model how to blend the second word, *Van*. **What kind of vehicle is the tan van?** (ice-cream truck)

**page 3** **Put your finger on the word that tells what Zig Pig did.** (ran) **Why did Zig do that?**

**page 4** **Now we know the name of the other main character. Who will read it for us?** (Dan Cat) **What did he ask for?**

**page 5** **Point to the word that tells what the characters did when they got their ice-cream cones.** (sat) **What other word here rhymes with sat?** (Cat) **What letters are the same in those rhyming words?** (a, t as in at)

**Purposes**
- apply phonics skills
- apply high-frequency words

**Tan Van**
by Amy Griffin
illustrated by Amiko Hirao

9

It is a tan van!

10

Zig Pig ran.
Can I have it?

11

Dan Cat ran.
Can I have it?

12

Zig Pig sat.
Dan Cat sat.

13

**DAY 3**

### Home Connection

Children can color the pictures in the take-home version of "Tan Van." After rereading on Day 4, they can take it home to read to family members.

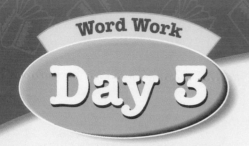

# Building Words

▶ **Word Family: –*ig***

Remind children that they know all the sounds and letters to build the word *dig*. Model how to build the word with Letter Cards. *Listen as I stretch out the sounds: / d / / ĭ / / g /. How many sounds do you hear? The first sound is / d /. I'll put up a* d *to spell that. The next sound is / ĭ /. What letter should I choose for that? The last sound is / g /. What letter spells / g /?*

Blend / d /, / ĭ /, and / g / and read *dig*. Then tell children you want to build a word that rhymes with *dig*. Replace *d* with *f* and say: *Now what happens if I change / d / to / f /?* Continue making and blending -*ig* words by substituting *b, r, p,* and *z.*

Have small groups work together to build -*ig* words. They can use letter tiles or other manipulative letters in your collection.

# Shared Writing

## ▶ Writing a Class Story

**Listening** Review that stories usually have three important parts: a beginning, a middle, and an end. Explain that we often read about the characters' problem at the beginning of a story. Reread a few pages of *Vroom, Chugga, Vroom-Vroom.* Ask what the racers did at the beginning and what their problem was. (They were getting ready to race and all wanted to win!)

Invite children to help you write a class story.

- What kind of vehicle would they like to write about? List children's suggestions on chart paper. Then have them vote on one type.

- What problems might the vehicle have in the beginning? Help children brainstorm ideas. List them on a chart, and have the class vote for one.

Incorporate children's suggestions in a shared writing experience. After introducing the character and its problem, tell children that tomorrow they will help you write about what happens next and think of a good solution.

**OBJECTIVES**

**Children**
- plan a beginning for a class story

**MATERIALS**

- **Big Book:** *Vroom, Chugga, Vroom-Vroom*

DAY 3

Learning to Read

# Day 4

## Day at a Glance

### Learning to Read

**Big Book:**

***Cool Wheels***

✓ **Phonics: Reviewing /z/; Blending *-ig* words,** *page T98*

### Word Work

**Building Words,** *page T100*

### Writing & Language

**Interactive Writing,** *page T101*

**Half-Day Kindergarten**

✓ Indicates lessons for tested skills. Choose additional activities as time allows.

# Opening

## Calendar

| Sunday | Monday | Tuesday | Wednesday | Thursday | Friday | Saturday |
|---|---|---|---|---|---|---|
| | | | 1 | 2 | 3 | 4 |
| 5 | 6 | 7 | 8 | 9 | 10 | 11 |
| 12 | 13 | 14 | 15 | 16 | 17 | 18 |
| 19 | 20 | 21 | 22 | 23 | 24 | 25 |
| 26 | 27 | 28 | 29 | 30 | 31 | |

Talk about the positions of numbers on the calendar. ***What number comes* before *11? What number comes* after *11? Find 15. What two numbers is it* between? *What number is* above *15?* below?**

## Daily Message

**Modeled Writing** Use words more than once in the daily message. Then call on volunteers to find and match words that are the same.

Yesterday we had a book about make-believe race cars.
Today we will read a book about real vehicles.

## Word Wall

Distribute cards for the words on the Word Wall. Have children take turns matching their cards to the same words on the wall and asking the class to chant its spelling: **h-a-v-e *spells* have; a-n-d *spells* and.**

# Routines

## Daily Phonemic Awareness
### Blending Phonemes

Play a game with children.

- *Listen as I say some sounds. You blend the sounds to make words we use to tell where. Listen: /ŏ/ /n/ (on). That's right, on. Say it with me: /ŏ/ /n/, on.*

- Continue with other one-syllable position words.

### Position Words

| | | |
|---|---|---|
| in | next | right |
| top | left | front |
| up | back | down |

## Getting Ready to Learn

To help plan their day, tell children that they will

- read the Science Link: *Cool Wheels.*

- learn to make and read words with -*ig*.

- read a book called "Tan Van."

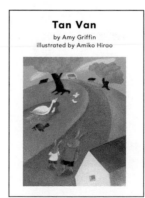

### Big Book

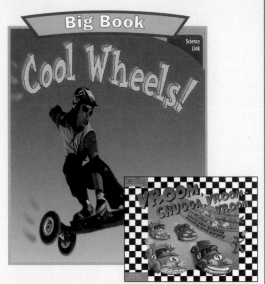

pages 33–39

## Oral Language

**scooter** A *scooter* is a motor bike—a bike with a motor. A scooter is like a motorcycle but smaller.

### English Language Learners

Ask children if they have ever heard the word *cool*. Ask, *What do you think cool means?* Tell them that it has several meanings. It can mean *chilly,* or *cold,* but in this article it means *special.*

# Sharing the Big Book
## *Science Link*

## ▶ Building Background

Display the title page for *Cool Wheels* and read it aloud. *Have you ever seen wheels like these? What do these wheels look like?* (skateboard with wagon wheels) *What do you think "cool" means?* Invite children to tell about other wheels they think are "cool."

**Reading for Understanding** Pause for discussion as you share the selection.

### page 33

### Strategy: Monitor/Clarify

**Student Modeling** *Is there anything about the title or this picture that confuses you? If so, what could you do to understand it better?* (look at the pictures; reread or read on; ask for help)

### pages 34–35

### Comprehension Focus: Cause and Effect

**Student Modeling** Remind children that sometimes one thing causes another thing to happen. Ask: *What makes a skateboard and a skate go?* (Person uses leg power to push off and move the wheels; going downhill causes wheels to roll on their own.)

### pages 36–37

### Compare and Contrast

- *How is what makes a bike go different from what makes a wheelchair go? What is the same? ... How is this wheelchair different from wheelchairs you have seen?*

### page 38

### Drawing Conclusions

- *Why is it important to wear helmets and other safety equipment when riding these cool wheels?*

### page 39

### Making Judgments

- *Have you seen some cool wheels? What makes them special?*

A skateboard has wheels. What makes it go?

A skate has wheels. What makes it go?

34

35

**pages 34–35**

A bike has wheels. What makes it go?

A wheelchair has wheels. What makes it go?

36

37

**pages 36–37**

A scooter has wheels. What makes it go?

Do you have some cool wheels? What makes them go?

38

39

**pages 38–39**

pages 34–35

## Concepts of Print

 Match Words in Print

■ Read aloud page 34. Frame the word *has* and identify it. Call on volunteers to find the same word on page 35. ***How do you know the words are the same?*** Continue with other words that are repeated on the two pages: *A, wheels, What, makes, it, go.*

## ▶ Responding

**Summarizing** Say that the author thinks many wheels are special, and ask children to name them. Which wheels did they like best? Why?

**DAY 4**

**Challenge**
MEETING INDIVIDUAL NEEDS

For children who are ready for a challenge, prepare cards for the words and end marks in one or two sentences from the selection. One child builds a sentence and then challenges a partner to read it and find it in the book.

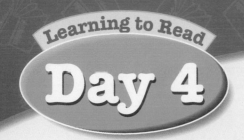

## OBJECTIVES

**Children**

- identify initial *z* for words that begin with /z/

- blend *z* and other initial consonants with *-ig*

## MATERIALS

- ***From Apples to Zebras: A Book of ABCs,*** page 27

- **Alphafriend Card** *Iggy Iguana*

- **Letter Cards** *b, d, f, g, i, l, p, r, z*

- **Punctuation Cards:** period, question mark

- **Phonics Center:** Theme 7, Week 2, Day 4

## Teacher's Note

During writing, children may ask how to spell words from the *-ig* family. Help children find *dig* on the Word Wall and substitute the appropriate initial consonant(s).

# Phonics

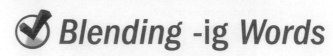

## ✓ *Blending -ig Words*

### ▶ Connect Sounds to Letters

**Review Consonant *z*** Using self-stick notes, cover the words on page 27 of *From Apples to Zebras: A Book of ABC's*. Then display the page. Ask what letter children expect to see first in each word and why. Uncover the words so children can check their predictions.

**Reviewing *-ig*** Ask if children remember which Alphafriend stands for the vowel sound /ĭ/. Display Iggy Iguana and have children name other words that start with /ĭ/. (*into, igloo, itch, instrument*)

***Now watch and listen as I build* dig: /d//ĭ//g/, dig, /d//ĭ//g/, dig.**

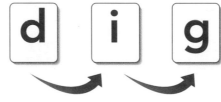 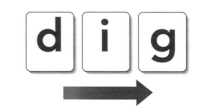

**Blending *-ig* Words** Replace the *d* with Letter Card *z*. ***Now let's blend my new word:* /z//ig/, zig.** Continue, choosing children to build and blend *pig, big, fig,* and *rig*. Monitor responses to see who needs more help.

## ▶ Apply

Begin a sentence with the three Word Cards shown. For *big* and *pig*, ask what letter you need to spell each sound. Build the words with Letter Cards.

Repeat the activity with *Can a <Picture Card: dog> dig?*

**Practice Book page 211** Children will complete this page at small group time.

**Phonics Library** In groups today, children will also read *-ig* words as they reread the **Phonics Library** story "Tan Van." See suggestions, page T91.

### At Group Time

### Phonics Center

Use Phonics Center materials for **Theme 7, Week 2, Day 4**.

---

**Practice Book p. 211**

Name _____

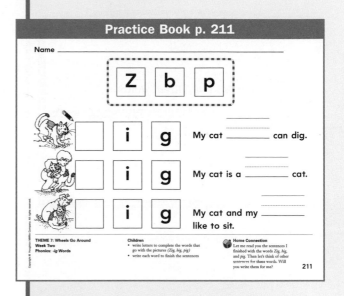

My cat _____ can dig.

My cat is a _____ cat.

My cat and my _____ like to sit.

THEME 7: Wheels Go Around
Week Two
Phonics: -ig Words

Children
• write letters to complete the words that go with the pictures (Zig, big, pig)
• write each word to finish the sentences

Home Connection
Let me read you the sentences I finished with the words Zig, big, and pig. Then let's think of other sentences for these words. Will you write them for me?

211

**Portfolio Opportunity**

Save children's Practice Book pages and other writing samples for their portfolios.

### Diagnostic Check

| If . . . | You can . . . |
|---|---|
| children have trouble building words and sentences, | have them work with you or a partner. |
| children can easily build words and sentences, | have them work with partners to build original sentences with *-ig* words. |

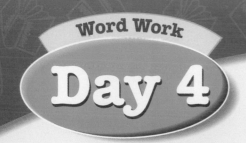
### OBJECTIVES

**Children**

- build and read *-ig, -it, -at* words

### MATERIALS

- **Letter Cards** *a, b, c, d, f, g, h, i, l, m, p, r, s, t, v, z*

# Building Words

## ▶ Word Families: *-ig, -it, -at*

Remind children that they have learned to build words by blending sounds together. Demonstrate by building *dig* in the pocket chart, stretching out the sounds.

Remove the *d.* **Let's build the word** **pig.** **Which letter should I put in front of** -ig? Continue with other letters children have learned (*b, f, r, z*) to build more *-ig* words.

Next, use Letter Cards to build *it.* **Listen:** /ĭ/ /t/. **How many sounds do you hear? ...What letter spells the sound** /ĭ/? **The last sound is** /t/. **What letter spells that sound?** Blend /ĭ/ and /t/ to read *it.*

Continue building words with initial consonants:

- Ask which letter you should add to build *lit*. Model how to read *lit* by blending /l/ with /it/.

- Replace *l* with *p*. **What happens if I change** /l/ to /p/? Continue making and blending *it* words by substituting *f, h, s, z.*

- Repeat, this time building *-at* and making new words by substituting initial consonants *b, c, f, h, m, p, r, s.*

Have children build some *-ig, -it,* and *-at* words with magnetic letters. Children can list the words they make onto paper and read their lists to a partner.

 **Challenge**

Children who can blend words with *-ig* easily can build a personal word bank of *-ig* words in their journals.

# Interactive Writing

## ▶ Writing a Class Story

Together, reread the beginning of the story children helped to develop in yesterday's shared writing. (See page T93.)

■ Review that the beginning of a story usually tells about the main character's problem. Have children name their story character and its problem.

■ Next, have children brainstorm ways the problem might be solved. List ideas on a chart. Then have the class vote on one to write about. (Save other ideas for future stories!)

■ Have children dictate the story, one line at a time. As you write the story, skip lines on the chart paper to allow room for additions and changes.

■ Occasionally, call on volunteers to write initial or final consonants, spell high-frequency words, or help you build words belonging to known word families.

■ Reread the story together.

**Portfolio Opportunity**

Occasionally make photocopies of individual pages a child contributes to a class writing project and add them to the portfolio.

## At Group Time

### Writing Center

Post today's work in the Writing Center. Children can choose the beginning, middle, or end of the story, draw an illustration on art paper, and add a caption. Recopy the story onto sheets of drawing paper and bind them together with the illustrations to form a class book.

Little Tow Truck

One day a fire ... the

No one wanted Little Tow Truck. He was too little.

Little Tow Truck pulled and pulled. He did it!

DAY 4

# Day 5

## Day at a Glance

### Learning to Read

**Revisiting the Literature:**

*The Little Engine That Could, Vroom, Chugga, Vroom-Vroom, Cool Wheels!* and *"Tan Van"*

✓ **Phonics: Review Blending Consonants; *-ig, -it, -an* words; *page T106***

### Word Work

**Building Words,** *page T108*

### Writing & Language

**Independent Writing,** *page T109*

---

**Half-Day Kindergarten**

✓ Indicates lessons for tested skills. Choose additional activities as time allows.

---

# Opening

## Calendar

| Sunday | Monday | Tuesday | Wednesday | Thursday | Friday | Saturday |
|--------|--------|---------|-----------|----------|--------|----------|
|  |  |  | 1 | 2 | 3 | 4 |
| 5 | 6 | 7 | 8 | 9 | 10 | 11 |
| 12 | 13 | 14 | 15 | 16 | 17 | 18 |
| 19 | 20 | 21 | 22 | 23 | 24 | 25 |
| 26 | 27 | 28 | 29 | 30 | 31 |  |

rainy day

sunny day

snowy day

Have children compare this week's weather with last week's. *How many days had sunny (rainy, snowy, overcast) weather last week? this week? Which week had more (fewer) days like that?*

## Daily Message

**Interactive Writing** Write about your plans for the weekend and invite children to share theirs. Have children spell or write their own names and supply familiar initial consonants for words.

Pat will visit her grandma.

Raul can help his dad wash the van.

Read the Word Wall together. Then play a rhyming game: *I see a word on the wall that rhymes with* fig. *The word is* dig. *Now raise your hand when you find a word that rhymes with* door. (for)

# Routines

 ## Daily Phonemic Awareness
### Blending Phonemes

- Display in random order the Picture Cards *dog, hog, log, pit, kit, lip,* and *zip.*

- *I will say some sounds. You blend the sounds together and raise your hand when you know which Picture Card I named: /l/ /ŏ/ /g/.*

- When most hands are up, ask children to say the word aloud with you. *That's right! /l/ /ŏ/ /g/, log.* If children mistakenly say *hog* or *dog,* repeat the sounds and emphasize /l/.

- Continue until all the Picture Cards have been named.

## Getting Ready to Learn

**To help plan their day, tell children that they will**

- reread and talk about all the books they've shared this week.

- take home a story they can read.

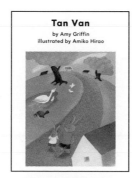

- write in their journals.

DAY 5

**Tan Van**
by Amy Griffin
illustrated by Amiko Hirao

# Revisiting the Literature

## ▶ Literature Discussion

Tell children that today they will compare the selections you shared this week. First, help children recall them:

■ Have volunteers tell what happened in the beginning, in the middle, and at the end of *The Little Engine That Could.*

■ Take a picture walk through *Vroom, Chugga, Vroom-Vroom,* and have children take turns telling what happened in the race.

■ Have children tell what is special about the *Cool Wheels!* as they discuss the photographs.

■ On the board write *Zig Pig*, the name of a character in "Tan Van." Ask volunteers how they blended the sounds to read the name.

■ Ask children to vote for their favorite book of the week. Then read aloud the winner.

## Comprehension: Cause and Effect

**Comparing Books** Remind children that in stories *and* in real life, one event can cause something to happen. Browse through each selection together, point out an appropriate event, and have children tell what caused it.

**Technology**

## www.eduplace.com
Log on to **Education Place** for more activities relating to Wheels Go Around.

## www.bookadventure.org
This Internet reading incentive program provides thousands of titles for children to read.

# Building Fluency

## ▶ Rereading Familiar Texts

**Phonics Library: "Tan Van"** Remind children that they've learned the new word *have* and that they've learned to read words with *-ig*. As children reread the **Phonics Library** story "Tan Van," have them look for *-ig* words.

**Review** Feature several familiar **Phonics Library** titles in the Book Corner. Have children demonstrate their growing skills by choosing one to reread aloud, alternating pages with a partner. From time to time, ask children to point out words or pages that they can read more easily now.

**Oral Reading** Model how to read the questions in "Tan Van" as Zig Pig and Dan Cat might have said them. Then have children try it.

**Tan Van**
by Amy Griffin
illustrated by Amiko Hirao

**Big Rig**
by Amy Griffin
illustrated by Bob Kolar

**Fan**
by Amy Griffin
illustrated by Dagmar Fehlau

**Blackline Master 36** Children complete the page and take it home to share their reading progress.

**My Reading Log**

I can read

My new words

have   dig

### Leveled Books

The materials listed below provide reading practice for children at different levels.

**Little Big Books**

**Little Readers for Guided Reading**

**Houghton Mifflin Classroom Bookshelf**

**Home Connection**

Remind children to share the **take-home** version of "Tan Van" with their families.

**DAY 5**

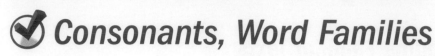

# Phonics Review

## ☑ Consonants, Word Families

### OBJECTIVES

**Children**

- build and read words with initial consonants and short *a* + *t*, short *a* + *n*, short *i* + *t*, short *i* + *g*
- make sentences with high-frequency words

### MATERIALS

- **Word Cards** *a, for, have, I, my*
- **Picture Cards** *dog, leash*
- **Punctuation Card:** period

## ▶ Review

Tell children they will take turns being word builders and word readers. Have a group of word builders stand with you at the chalkboard.

■ *Let's build the word* dig. *First, count the sounds: /d / /ĭ / /g /. I know* d *stands for /d /,* i *stands for /ĭ /, and* g *stands for /g /. Let's write the letters.*

■ Replace *d* with *p*. The word builders do the same and ask the rest of the class (word readers) what new word was made.

■ Have a new group of word builders come to the board. At your direction, they erase the *p*, write *b*, and ask the word readers to say the new word. Continue the activity with *zig* and *fig*.

■ Now challenge children to show what letter they should replace to change *fig* to *fit*. Continue with *bit, pit, quit, hit; hat, mat, fat; fan, Nan, van.*

# High-Frequency Word Review

☑️ *I, see, my, like, a, to, and, go, for, have*

## ▶ Review

Give each small group the Word Cards, Picture Cards, and Punctuation Card needed to make a sentence. Each child holds one card. Children stand and arrange themselves to make a sentence for others to read. After the class reads the sentence, have them act it out.

## ▶ Apply

**Practice Book page 212** Children can complete this page independently and read it to you during small group time.

**Phonics Library** Have children take turns reading aloud to the class. Each child might read one page of "Tan Van," "Big Rig," or a favorite **Phonics Library** selection from a previous week. Remind readers to share the pictures!

Questions for discussion:

- *Do you hear any rhyming words in either story? What letters are the same in those words?*

- *Find a word that starts with the same sound as Zelda Zebra's name. What is the letter? What is the sound?*

- *This week we added the word* have *to the Word Wall. Find* have *in "Tan Van."*

**Practice Book p. 212**

Name _____

have  for  is  Here

1. I ____ a big fig.
2. Is it ____ Pig?
3. It ____ for Pig and Cat.
4. ____ is a big fig. A big fig

THEME 7: Wheels Go Around
Week Two
High-Frequency Words Review have, for, is, here

Children
• read the speech balloons
• write a word from the box to complete what the characters are saying
• color the pictures

Home Connection
Let me read this cartoon to you. Then maybe you can read a newspaper cartoon to me.

212

## 🧰 Portfolio Opportunity

Save the Practice Book page to show children's recognition of high-frequency words.

### Diagnostic Check ✓

| If . . . | You can . . . |
| --- | --- |
| children need help remembering the consonant sounds, | show how these letters' *names* give clues to their *sounds*. |
| children pause at high-frequency words in *Phonics Library* selections, | have partners use flash cars to practice word recognition. |

DAY 5

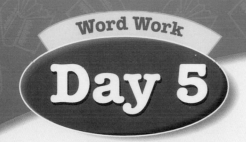

# Day 5

## OBJECTIVES

**Children**

- build and read -at, -an, -it, and -ig words

## MATERIALS

- **Letter Cards** *a, b, c, d, f, g, h, i, l, m, n, p, qu, r, s, t, v, z*

# Building Words

## ▶ Word Families: -at, -an, -it, -ig

Model how to build *it*. Along the bottom of the pocket chart, line up the letters *b, f, h, l, p, qu,* and *s*. ***I want to build the word* lit. *Who can tell me which letter I should take from here to make* lit?*** Have a volunteer take the letter *l* and place it in front of *-it*. Continue building *-it* words, using initial consonants *b, f, h, p, qu,* and *s*. On chart paper, keep a list of all the *-it* words you make, and reread the list together.

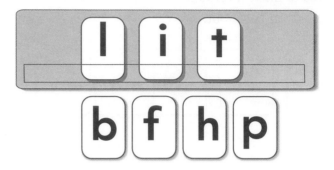

Continue the activity with *-an, -at, and -ig* words. Examples: *can, Dan, fan, man; bat, cat, Pat, rat, vat; big, pig, rig, zig.*

Have small groups work together to build *-it, -an, -at,* and *-ig* words with magnetic letters or other materials. This time, they can write some of the new words in the Word Bank section of their journals and add pictures.

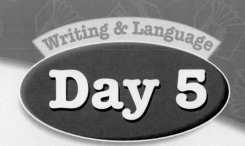

# Independent Writing

**Journals** Together, reread the class story you composed this week. Then recall your discussions about trains, race cars, and other vehicles.

■ Pass out the journals.

■ *Let's think about some of the things we learned this week. What kind of wheels could you write about? What did you learn about the beginning of a story? Maybe you'll decide to draw a vehicle that has a problem and then write about it.*

■ Remind children that they can use words from Word Wall as well as the charts with words that tell where. Remind children to use what they know about letter sounds to help them spell other words.

■ If time permits, allow children to share what they've written with the class.

I think I can too!

Vroom-vroom, zoom.

## OBJECTIVES

**Children**
• write independently

## MATERIALS

• journals

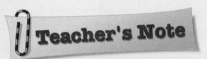

### Teacher's Note

Suggest that children browse through *Vroom, Chugga, Vroom-Vroom* and *Cool Wheels!* for writing ideas.

### Portfolio Opportunity

Mark journal entries you would like to share with parents. Occasionally ask children to mark their best efforts or favorite works for sharing as well.

**DAY 5**

# Literature for Week 3

## Different texts for different purposes

## Teacher Read Alouds:
- **Wheels Around**
- **The Little Engine That Could**
- **Mr. Gumpy's Motor Car**

### Purposes
- oral language
- listening strategy
- comprehension

## Big Books:

### Higglety Pigglety: A Book of Rhymes

#### Purposes
- oral language development
- phonemic awareness

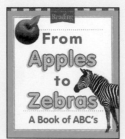

### From Apples to Zebras: A Book of ABC's

#### Purposes
- alphabet recognition
- letters and sounds

## Big Book: Main Selections

### Purposes
- concepts of print
- reading strategy
- story language
- comprehension skills

**Also available in Little Big Book and audiotape**

**Also available in Little Big Book and audiotape**

# Leveled Books

## On My Way Paperback

**Dig, Zig Pig!**
*by* **Sam Fonte**
page T155

## Little Readers for Guided Reading
Collection K

## Houghton Mifflin Classroom Bookshelf
Level K

**Technology**

### www.eduplace.com
Log on to *Education Place* for more activities relating to *Wheels Go Around*.

### www.bookadventure.org
This free Internet reading incentive program provides thousands of titles for students to read.

## Also in the Big Books:
**– Science Link**

### Purposes
- reading strategies
- comprehension skills
- concepts of print

### Phonics Library

Also available in Take-Home version

**Wheels Go Around**

### Purposes
- applying phonics skills and high-frequency words

# Suggested Daily Routines

## Instructional Goals

### Learning to Read

✔ *Phonemic Awareness:* Blending Phonemes

*Strategy Focus:* Question, Summarize

✔ *Comprehension Skill:* Making Predictions

✔ *Phonics Skills*

*Phonemic Awareness:* Beginning Sounds /d/, /z/

Initial Consonants *D, d* and *Z, z;* Short *i* + *g*

*Compare and Review:* Initial Consonant: *r*

✔ *High-Frequency Words:* for, have

✔ *Concepts of Print:* Match Spoken Words to Print; Match Words

### Word Work

*High-Frequency Word Practice:*
Word Families: *-ig, -it, -at*

### Writing & Language

*Vocabulary Skills:* Using Opposites, Words for Travel

*Writing Skill:* Writing a Report

✔ = tested skills

### Leveled Books

*Have children read in appropriate levels daily.*

**Phonics Library**
**On My Way Practice Readers**
**Little Big Books**
**Houghton Mifflin Classroom Bookshelf**

## Day 1

**Opening Routines,** *T116–T117*

Word Wall
• Phonemic Awareness: Blending Phonemes

**Teacher Read Aloud**
*Mr. Gumpy's Motor Car, T118–T121*
• **Strategy:** Question
• **Comprehension:** Making Predictions

### Phonics
**Instruction**
• Phonemic Awareness, Beginning Sound /d/, /z/, T122–T123; *Practice Book, 215–216*

**High-Frequency Word Practice**
• Words: *a, for, have, I, my, T124*

**Oral Language**
• Using Opposites, *T125*
• Listening and Speaking, *T125*

**Managing Small Groups**
**Teacher-Led Group**
• Reread familiar **Phonics Library** selections

**Independent Groups**
• Finish *Practice Book, 213–216*
• *Phonics Center:* Theme 7, Week 3, Day 1
• Book, Dramatic Play, Writing, other Centers

## Day 2

**Opening Routines,** *T126–T127*

Word Wall
• Phonemic Awareness: Blending Phonemes

**Sharing the Big Book**
*The Wheels on the Bus, T128–T129*
• **Strategy:** Question
• **Comprehension:** Making Predictions

### Phonics
**Instruction, Practice**
• Review Initial Consonants *d, z, T130–T131*
• *Practice Book, 217*

**High-Frequency Words**
• Review Words: *for, have, T132–T133*
• *Practice Book, 218*

**High-Frequency Word Practice**
• Building Sentences, *T134*

**Vocabulary Expansion**
• Words for Travel, *T135*

**Managing Small Groups**
**Teacher-Led Group**
• Begin *Practice Book, 217–218* and handwriting Blackline Masters 160 or 186 and 182 or 208.

**Independent Groups**
• Finish *Practice Book, 217–218* and handwriting Blackline Masters 160 or 186 and 182 or 208.
• *Phonics Center:* Theme 7, Week 3, Day 2
• Writing, Art, other Centers

Technology

**Lesson Planner CD-ROM:** Customize your planning for *Wheels Go Around* with the Lesson Planner.

# Day 3

**Opening Routines,** *T136–T137*

- **Phonemic Awareness:** Blending Phonemes

**Sharing the Big Book**
*Vroom, Chugga, Vroom-Vroom, T138–T139*
- **Strategy:** Question
- **Comprehension:** Making Predictions, *T138; Practice Book, 219*
- **Concepts of Print:** Match Spoken Words to Print; Match Words, *T139*

## Phonics
**Practice, Application**
- Review Consonants *d* and *z*, *T140–T141*

**Instruction**
- Blending *d -ig, z -ig, T140–T141; Practice Book, 220*
- **Phonics Library:** "Zig Pig and Dan Cat," *T141*

**Building Words**
- Word Family: *-ig, T142*

✏️ **Shared Writing**
- Writing a Report, *T143*

### Managing Small Groups
**Teacher-Led Group**
- Read "Zig Pig and Dan Cat"
- Write letters *I, i;* begin **Blackline Masters 165 or 191.**
- Begin *Practice Book, 219–220*

**Independent Groups**
- Finish **Blackline Masters 165 or 191** and *Practice Book, 219–220.*
- Art, other Centers

# Day 4

**Opening Routines,** *T144–T145*

- **Phonemic Awareness:** Blending Phonemes

**Sharing the Big Book**
**Science Links:** "Look for Wheels,"
"Cool Wheels!," *T146–T147*
- **Strategy:** Summarize
- **Comprehension:** Making Predictions
- **Concepts of Print:** Match Spoken Words to Print; Match Words

## Phonics
**Practice**
- Blending *-ig* Words, *T148–T149; Practice Book, 221*

**Building Words**
- Word Families: *-ig, -it, -at, T150*

✏️ **Interactive Writing**
- Writing a Report, *T151*
- Viewing and Speaking, *T151*

### Managing Small Groups
**Teacher-Led Group**
- Reread **Phonics Library** selection "Zig Pig and Dan Cat"
- Begin *Practice Book, 221*

**Independent Groups**
- Finish *Practice Book, 221*
- *Phonics Center:* Theme 7, Week 3, Day 4
- Art, Writing, other Centers

# Day 5

**Opening Routines,** *T152–T153*

- **Phonemic Awareness:** Blending Phonemes

**Revisiting the Literature**
**Comprehension:** Making Predictions, *T154*

**Building Fluency**
- **On My Way Practice Reader:** "Dig, Zig Pig!," *T155*

## Phonics
**Review**
- Familiar Consonants; *-at, -an, -ig, -it, T156*

**High-Frequency Word Review**
- Words: *I, see, my, like, a, to, and, go, is, here, for, have, T157; Practice Book, 222*

**Building Words**
- Word Families: *-ig , -an, -it, T158*

✏️ **Independent Writing**
- Journals: Favorite Kind of Wheels, *T159*

### Managing Small Groups
**Teacher-Led Group**
- Reread familiar **Phonics Library** selections
- Begin *Practice Book, 222*, **Blackline Master 36.**

**Independent Groups**
- Reread **Phonics Library** selections
- Finish *Practice Book, 222*, **Blackline Master 36.**
- Centers

# Setting up the Centers

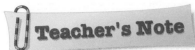 

Set an egg timer to go off when children should begin to clean up their Centers. You might also announce clean-up time with a lively chant:
Clean your Center for today.
Clean up, clean up, right away!

## Phonics Center

**Materials** • Phonics Center materials for Theme 7, Week 3

This week children sort pictures for inital sounds /d/, /r/, and /z/. They make words with the letters *b, d, p,* and the word family *-ig.* They also build sentences with Word and Picture Cards. Prepare materials for Days 1, 2, and 4. See pages T123, T131, and T149 for this week's Phonics Center activities.

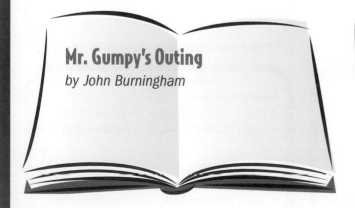

**Mr. Gumpy's Outing**
by John Burningham

## Book Center

**Materials** • *Mr. Gumpy's Outing*

Read aloud *Mr. Gumpy's Outing* and put a copy of it in the Book Center. See the Teacher's Note on page T119 for this week's Book Center suggestion.

# Writing Center

**Materials** • lined and unlined writing paper • drawing paper • crayons or markers

Children illustrate and label a pair of opposites. They draw and write about jobs they would enjoy. Later they draw pictures with captions to go with a class report. See pages T125, T139, and T151 for this week's Writing Center activities.

I can put out fires.

I can tell you to go and stop.

# Dramatic Play Center

**Materials** • Blackline Masters 108–109 • yarn

Children dramatize *Mr. Gumpy's Motor Car*, retelling the story or providing sound effects. See page T119 for this week's Dramatic Play Center activity.

# Art Center

**Materials** • drawing paper • crayons and markers

Children draw and label pictures of wheels at work, their favorite vehicle, and their own favorite "cool wheels." See pages T129, T135, and T147 for this week's Art Center activities.

I like my skates.

## Learning to Read

# Day 1

## Day at a Glance

### Learning to Read

**Teacher Read Aloud**

*Mr Gumpy's Motor Car*

☑ Phonics: Reviewing /d/, /z/, page T122

### Word Work

☑ **High-Frequency Word Practice,** page T124

### Writing & Language

**Oral Language,** *page T125*

---

 **Half-Day Kindergarten**

☑ Indicates lessons for tested skills. Choose additional activities as time allows.

---

# Opening

## Calendar

| Sunday | Monday | Tuesday | Wednesday | Thursday | Friday | Saturday |
|---|---|---|---|---|---|---|
| | | | 1 | 2 | 3 | 4 |
| 5 | 6 | 7 | 8 | 9 | 10 | 11 |
| 12 | 13 | 14 | 15 | 16 | 17 | 18 |
| 19 | 20 | 21 | 22 | 23 | 24 | 25 |
| 26 | 27 | 28 | 29 | 30 | 31 | |

wet/dry   hot/cold   cloudy/clear   rainy/sunny   day/night

After children describe the day's weather, talk about *opposites*, or things that are completely different. Suggest an opposite for today's weather. For example, if today is *rainy*, say that the opposite weather would be *sunny*. Continue withs: *day/night, hot/cold, wet/dry, mild/wild, dark/light, cloudy/clear.*

## Daily Message

**Modeled Writing** Tie today's message to the theme by asking if any children traveled on wheels over the weekend. As children tell about the vehicles, incorporate the responses into the day's message.

Kendra and Jamal rode on a bus. Sandy, Marco, and Alyssa rode on a subway train.

Choose a volunteer to point to and read the two words that were added to the Word Wall in this theme. *(for, have)* **Who can read the other word in the h column?** *(here)* Continue reading the other word groups.

# Routines

 **Daily Phonemic Awareness**
### Blending Phonemes

- Read "Hey, Diddle, Diddle" on page 32 of *Higglety Pigglety*.

- Play a guessing game. *I'll say some sounds. You put them together to make words from the poem:* /c/ /ă/ /t/ (cat); /d/ /ĭ/ /sh/ (dish); /r/ /ă/ /n/ (ran).

- Continue with other one-syllable words.

**Hey, Diddle, Diddle**

Hey, diddle, diddle!
The cat and the fiddle,
The cow jumped over the moon.
The little dog laughed
To see such sport,
And the dish ran away
With the spoon.

a Mother Goose Rhyme

*Higglety Pigglety: A Book of Rhymes*, page 32

## Getting Ready to Learn

To help plan their day, tell children that they will

- listen to a story called *Mr. Gumpy's Motor Car.*

- revisit two Alphafriends, Dudley Duck and Zelda Zebra.

- act out a story in the Dramatic Play Center.

# Day 1

**Purposes** • oral language • listening strategy
• comprehension skill

## Selection Summary
The sun is shining when Mr. Gumpy agrees to take his children and the animals for a car ride. But when the skies open up and the road turns muddy, it takes the help of all the passengers to free the car from the mud.

## Key Concepts
Many hands make easy work.

 **Teacher's Note**

**Read Aloud Tip** Give life and personality to the characters. Read the dialogue with expression.

# Teacher Read Aloud
## Oral Language/Comprehension

▶ **Building Background**

Explain that today's story is about a car. Invite children to tell about car rides they have shared with family or friends. *Were you taking a drive for fun or did you have a place to go to? How many people went for the ride? What was the weather like?*

 **Comprehension: Making Predictions**

**Teacher Modeling** Display the picture on T121 and read the title, *Mr. Gumpy's Motor Car.* Then model how to make predictions about the story.

> **Think Aloud**
>
> *The title tells me the story is about Mr. Gumpy's motor car. In the picture, I see a man and a car. The man must be Mr. Gumpy, and the motor car must be his. I also see that Mr. Gumpy is holding a case, so maybe he is going somewhere. I will read the story to find out if my prediction is right.*

## Strategy: Question

**Teacher Modeling** Model how to pose questions you'd like the story to answer.

> **Think Aloud**
>
> • *Asking questions before you read can help you understand a story better and make it even more interesting. I wonder: Where does Mr. Gumpy go on his car ride? Who does he take with him? Let's listen for the answers as I read.*

## ▶ Listening to the Story

Read the story with expression. As you read the long list of characters, count them off on your fingers and invite children to do the same. Pause for the discussion points, asking children to tell what might happen next. Read on to check their predictions. Note that the Read Aloud art is also available on the back of the Theme Poster.

## ▶ Responding

**Summarizing the Story** Use these prompts to help children summarize.

■ *What did Mr. Gumpy decide to do at the beginning of the story? Who wanted to come along?*

■ *What prediction did Mr. Gumpy make when he saw the clouds? Was he right? What happened next?*

■ *What reasons did the children and the animals give for not wanting to push the motor car? How did the car finally get out of the mud?*

■ *What do you think will happen the next time Mr. Gumpy needs help? Why?*

**Practice Book pages 213–214** Children will complete the pages during small group time.

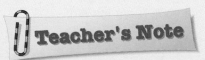

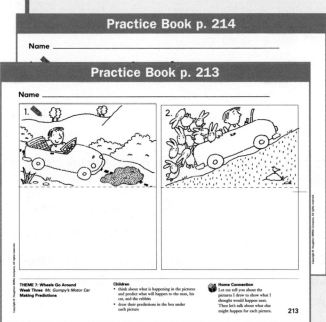

### At Group Time

## Dramatic Play Center

**Materials** • Blackline Masters 108–109

Give each child a character's picture from **Blackline Master 00**. Then use yarn to outline an area in the Center to be Mr. Gumpy's motor car. Children can hold the characters and crowd into the car for an afternoon drive across the fields. Reread the story, having children supply appropriate sound effects.

### Teacher's Note

Children who enjoyed this story may also enjoy another John Burningham book, *Mr. Gumpy's Outing*, a story about a boat ride that ends with a real splash.

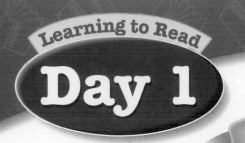
# Mr. Gumpy's Motor Car

### by John Burningham
### A Contemporary British Tale

r. Gumpy was going for a ride in his car. He drove out of the gate and down the lane.

"May we come too?" said the children.

"May we?" said the rabbit, the cat, the dog, the pig, the sheep, the chickens, the calf, and the goat.

"All right," said Mr. Gumpy. "But it will be a squash."

And they all piled in.

"It's a lovely day," said Mr. Gumpy. "Let's take the old dirt road across the fields."

For a while they drove along happily. The sun shone, the engine chugged, and everyone was enjoying the ride.

"I don't like the look of those clouds. I think it's going to rain," said Mr. Gumpy.

Very soon the dark clouds were right overhead. Mr. Gumpy stopped the car. He jumped out, put up the top, and down came the rain.

The road grew muddier and muddier, and the wheels began to spin. Mr. Gumpy looked at the hill ahead. (**Say:** *That sounds like trouble! What do you think Mr. Gumpy will do? Let's read on and find the answer.*)

"Some of you will have to get out and push," he said.

"Not me," said the goat. "I am too old."

"Not me," said the calf. "I am too young."

"Not us," said the chickens. "We can't push."

"Not me," said the sheep. "I might catch a cold."

"Not me," said the pig. "I've a bone in my trotter."

"Not me," said the dog. "But I'll drive if you like."

"Not me," said the cat. "It would ruin my fur."

"Not me," said the rabbit. "I'm not very well."

"Not me," said the girl. "He's stronger."

"Not me," said the boy. "She's bigger."(**Say:** *Oh, no! No one wanted to help! What will happen to the car?*)

The wheels churned...

The car sank deeper into the mud.

"Now we're really stuck," said Mr. Gumpy.

(**Ask:** *Were we right? Now I wonder how they will get out of this mess! Let's read on to find out.*)

They all got out and pushed.

They pushed and shoved and heaved and strained and gasped and slipped and slithered and squelched. Slowly the car began to move ...

"Don't stop!" cried Mr. Gumpy. "Keep it up! We're nearly there."

Everyone gave a mighty heave — the tires gripped ...

The car edged its way to the top of the hill. They looked up and saw that the sun was shining again. It began to get hot.

"We'll drive home across the bridge," said Mr. Gumpy. "Then you can go for a swim." And they did.

After a while it was time to go home.

"Good-bye," said Mr. Gumpy. "Come for a drive another day."

# Day 1

## OBJECTIVES

**Children**

- identify pictures whose names begin with /d/, /z/

## MATERIALS

- **Alphafriend Cards** *Dudley Duck, Reggie Rooster, Zelda Zebra*
- **Alphafriend Audiotape** Theme 7
- **Alphafolder** *Dudley Duck, Zelda Zebra*
- **Picture Cards** for *d, r, z*
- **Phonics Center:** Theme 7, Week 3, Day 1

### Home Connection

Take-home versions of the songs for Dudley Duck and Zelda Zebra are on **Alphafriends Blackline Masters.** Children can share the songs with their families.

# Phonemic Awareness
## ✓ Beginning Sound

▶ **Revisiting the Alphafriends: Dudley Duck, Zelda Zebra**

Adapt the Alphafriend routine to review Dudley Duck and Zelda Zebra.

**1 Alphafriend Riddles** Share these clues to recall the Alphafriends:

- *This Alphafriend's sound is /d/. He quacks and swims.* Call on children until they guess *duck.*

- *This Alphafriend's sound is /z/. She has black and white stripes.* Call on children until they guess *zebra.*

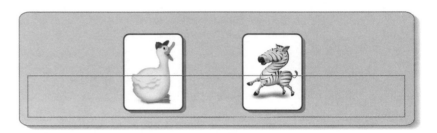

**2 Pocket Chart** Display *Dudley Duck* in the pocket chart. Say his name, emphasizing the /d/ sound and having children echo. Then display *Zelda Zebra*, stretching the /z/ sound as you say her name.

**3 Alphafriend Audiotape** Play Dudley Duck's song. Invite children to sing along and make "duck bills" when they hear words that start with /d/.

**4 Alphafriend Folder** Have children review the illustration and name the /d/ pictures.

**5 Summarize**

- *What is this Alphafriend's name? What is his sound?*

- *What words in his song start with /d/?*

- *What should we remember when we look at Dudley Duck?* (the /d/ sound)

Repeat Steps 3 through 5 to review Zelda Zebra's sound.

## ▶ Listening for /d/, /z/

**Compare and Review: /r/** Display Alphafriend *Reggie Rooster.* Review his sound.

Hold up the Picture Cards one at a time. Children signal "thumbs up" for picture names that start like Dudley's name and volunteers put those cards below Dudley's picture. For "thumbs down" words, volunteers put cards below the correct Alphafriend.

Pictures: *desk, zigzag, rock, doll, rope, zipper, rug, doll, zip.*

## ▶ Apply

**Practice Book page 215–216** Children will complete the pages at small group time.

### At Group Time

## Phonics Center

Use the Phonics Center materials for **Theme 7, Week 3, Day 1**.

## Word Work

# Day 1

## ▶ Matching Words

■ Display Word Cards for the high-frequency words *have* and *for* in a pocket chart. Call on children to identify each word and to match it on the Word Wall.

*Baa, Baa, Black Sheep*

Baa, baa, black sheep,
Have you any wool?
Yes, sir, yes, sir,
Three bags full,
One for the master,
One for the dame,
One for the little boy
Who lives in the lane.

a Mother Goose Rhyme

■ Remind children that these are words they often see in books. *I'll read a poem. You listen to hear if these words are in it.*

**Higglety Pigglety: A Book of Rhymes, page 16**

■ Read "Baa, Baa, Black Sheep" on page 16 of *Higglety Pigglety. Did you hear the words* have *and* for? Read the poem line for line and have volunteers match the Word Cards to those words in the poem.

**Writing Opportunity** In a pocket chart, display the Work and Practice cards from the Materials list. Begin a sentence with *I have*, and then ask volunteers to choose cards to complete the sentence in different ways. Distribute paper and have children write and illustrate one of the sentences or create their own.

# Oral Language

## ▶ Using Opposites

**Listening and Speaking** Remind children that the characters in *Mr. Gumpy's Motor Car* had different reasons for not wanting to push the car. **The goat said it was too old. The calf said it was too young. What do you know about the words old and young?** If necessary, explain that the words are *opposites*, or words that mean completely different things. Offer more examples: *wet/dry, cold/hot, out/in, on/off.*

■ Help children begin a list of opposites by rereading lines from the story that contain examples. List children's suggestions on a chart.

■ Use prompts to help children brainstorm more opposites. Examples: **What happens when a race car crosses the finish line first?** (It wins.) **What happens when it crosses last?** (It loses.)

**Portfolio Opportunity**
Save children's labeled drawings as a sample of their understanding of opposites and their writing abilities.

### Opposites

| | |
|---|---|
| old | young |
| rainy | sunny |
| stuck | loose |
| win | lose |
| fast | slow |
| full | empty |
| strong | weak |
| big | little |

**At Group Time**

# Writing Center

Put the chart in the Writing Center. Ask children to illustrate a pair of opposites and label their pictures.

big and little

# Day 2

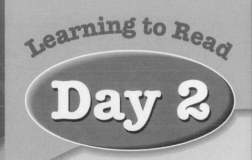

# Day at a Glance

## Learning to Read

**Big Book:**

*The Wheels on the Bus*

☑ **Phonics: Initial Consonants d, z,** page T130

☑ **High-Frequency Words:** *for, have,* page T132

## Word Work

**High-Frequency Word Practice,** page T134

## Writing & Language

**Vocabulary Expansion,** *page T135*

---

 **Half-Day Kindergarten**

☑ Indicates lessons for tested skills. Choose additional activities as time allows.

---

# Opening

## Calendar

| Sunday | Monday | Tuesday | Wednesday | Thursday | Friday | Saturday |
|---|---|---|---|---|---|---|
|  |  |  | 1 | 2 | 3 | 4 |
| 5 | 6 | 7 | 8 | 9 | 10 | 11 |
| 12 | 13 | 14 | 15 | 16 | 17 |  |
| 19 | 20 | 21 | 22 | 23 | 2 |  |
| 26 | 27 | 28 | 29 | 30 | 31 |  |

*sunny | rainy*
*first | last*

Play an opposites game after your calendar routine. Have a child say a word that describes today's weather and call on a classmate to say the word's opposite. Have other volunteers point to and name sections of the calendar such as *top, left* side, *first* day of the week, *first* date in the month; classmates can name the opposites.

## Daily Message

**Interactive Writing** As you write the daily message, have children help you. Ask them to supply initial and final consonants and to help you build and write *-ig* and *-it* words.

> It is sunny today, with big white clouds.

Distribute cards for the Word Wall words. Have children match their cards to the same words on the wall. After a match is made, have other children chant the spelling of the word: **a-n-d** *spells* **and;** **g-o** *spells* **go.**

# Routines

## Daily Phonemic Awareness
### Blending Phonemes

- Read "Humpty Dumpty" on page 19 of *Higglety Pigglety*.

- Play a guessing game. *I'll say some sounds. You put them together to make words from the poem: /s/ /ă/ /t/ (sat); /m/ /ě/ /n/ (men); /h/ /ă/ /d/ (had).*

- Continue with other one-syllable words.

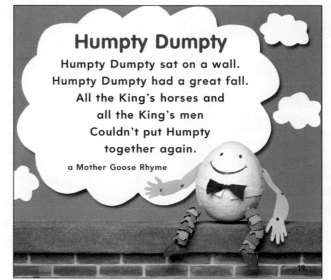

**Humpty Dumpty**

Humpty Dumpty sat on a wall.
Humpty Dumpty had a great fall.
All the King's horses and
all the King's men
Couldn't put Humpty
together again.

a Mother Goose Rhyme

*Higglety Pigglety: A Book of Rhymes*, page 19

## Getting Ready to Learn

To help plan their day, tell children that they will

- listen to a Big Book: *The Wheels on the Bus.*

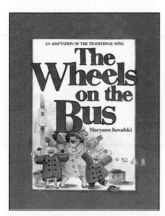

- review the letters *D, d* and *Z, z*, and sort words that begin with *d* and *z*.

- write about wheels in the Writing Center.

A 🚜 can help my dad.

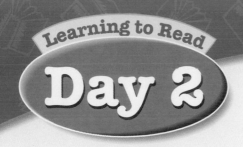

# Day 2

## Big Book

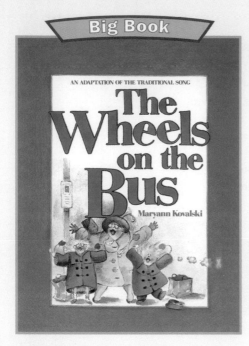

AN ADAPTATION OF THE TRADITIONAL SONG

# The Wheels on the Bus

Maryann Kovalski

**Purposes** • concepts of print • story language
• reading strategy • comprehension skill

**Extra Support**

On a rereading of the story, children can sing the text using the pictures as prompts.

# Sharing the Big Book
## Oral Language/Comprehension

### ▶ Building Background

Display *The Wheels on the Bus.* Call on volunteers to share what they remember about the story. *As we read the story this time, see if you can remember the things that happen on the old-fashioned bus.*

#### Strategy: Question

**Teacher-Student Modeling** *Asking yourself questions and then looking for the answers in the story is a good way to understand it better. I want to know why the characters don't see or hear the bus when it comes. I'll look for the answer when we read.* Ask children what questions *they* might ask about the characters or old-fashioned buses. Jot down their questions on chart paper and save them to answer after reading.

#### ✓ Comprehension Focus: Making Predictions

**Teacher-Student Modeling** Remind children that while reading, they can use picture clues and what they have read so far to tell what might happen next. Display the book cover and read the title. *What can you tell about this book from just the cover picture and the title?*

## ▶ Sharing the Story

Reread the story, pausing for these discussion points:

 **pages 2–3**

**Making Predictions**

■ *In the story Grandma took Jenny and Joanna shopping for new coats. What could you predict they would do after shopping?* (They would go back home.)

 **pages 12–13**

**Concepts of Print: Match spoken words to print; Match words**

■ *There's a word on the page for every word I say. Say each one with me as I point.*

■ Frame the word *and.* Ask children to say *and,* then find *and* three times. *What other words on these pages match? Show me and I'll read them for you.*

**pages 24–25**

**Strategy: Question**

■ *I see the real bus is here now. Look for the answer to my question: Why don't the characters see or hear that bus?*

## ▶ Responding

**Story Talk** Display the questions children posed before reading. Read each one and have children find the story page that shows the answer. Read the page and have children echo you.

**At Group Time**

# Writing Center

( **Materials** • drawing paper • crayons or markers )

Have children draw pictures of wheels that help people in their neighborhoods or towns. Children can complete this sentence stem to caption their drawings: *A _____ can help _____.*

A  can help my dad.

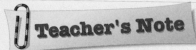

 **Teacher's Note**

To spark ideas, post an illustrated list of vehicle words in the Writing Center. Include vehicles commonly seen in your community. Some children will be able to use the words to label their drawings.

**Portfolio Opportunity**

Save children's writing for their portfolios.

**DAY 2**

**Challenge**

Small groups can work together to make books of wheels in their community. After drawing and captioning their pictures, have children decide whether any vehicles are missing. Then assemble the pages into a class book.

# Phonics

## ✓ Review Initial Consonants d, z

### ▶ Develop Phonemic Awareness

**Beginning Sounds** Read aloud the lyrics from Dudley Duck's song and have children echo it line-for-line. Have them listen for the /d/ words and pantomime a duck's bill for each one. Repeat for /z/ with Zelda Zebra's song, having children trace a zigzag motion in the air for each /z/.

### ▶ Connect Sounds to Letters

**Beginning Letters** Display the Alphafriends cards *Dudley Duck* and *Zelda Zebra*. Have children name the letters on the pictures. *What letter stands for the sound /d/, as in duck? What letter stands for the sound /z/, as in zebra? Which animal will help you remember the sound for d? the sound for z?*

Tell children you want to write *duck* on the board. *What letter should I write first? How did you know?* Repeat with the word *zebra*.

**Compare and Review: *d, z, r*** In the pocket chart, display the Letter Cards as shown and the Picture Cards in random order. Review the sounds for *d, z,* and *r*. In turn, children can name a picture, say the beginning sound, and put the card below the right letter.

Tell children they will sort more pictures today in the Phonics Center.

## ▶ Handwriting

**Writing *D, d; Z, z*** Remind children that they have learned how to write the letters that stand for / d /: capital *D* and small *d*. They have also learned how to write the letters for / z /: capital *Z* and small *z*. Ask children to write each letter in the air as you recite the handwriting rhymes together.

| Handwriting Rhyme: D | Handwriting Rhyme: d | Handwriting Rhyme: Z | Handwriting Rhyme: z |
|---|---|---|---|
| Big *D* starts with a long line down. Go back to the top and curve all the way around: It's a *D*, a big *D*! | Start in the middle. Make a circle nice and round. Go up to the top and come straight down: It's a *d*, a small *d*, a small *d*! | From the top, zip right with a line. Slant down to the left, and zip right one more time: It's a *Z*, big *Z*, big *Z*! | From the middle, zip right with a line. Slant down to the left, and zip right one more time: It's a *z*, a small *z*, small *z*! |

## ▶ Apply

**Practice Book page 217** Children will complete the page at small group time.

**Blackline Masters 160, 182** These pages provide additional handwriting practice for small group time.

### At Group Time

# Phonics Center

Use the Phonics Center Materials for **Theme 7, Week 3, Day 2**.

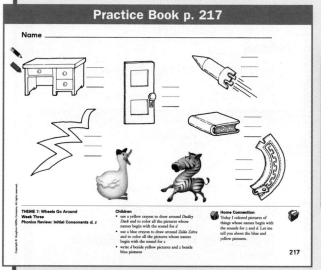
### Teacher's Note

Handwriting practice for the continuous stroke style is available on **Blackline Masters 186, 208.**

### Portfolio Opportunity

Save the **Practice Book** page to show children's grasp of the letter-sound associations.
Save **Blackline Masters 160, 182** for handwriting samples.

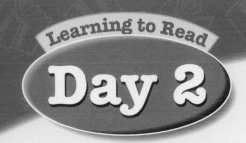
# ✓ High-Frequency Words

## *Review Words:* for, have

▶ **Teach**

Tell children that today they will practice reading and writing two words that they will see often in stories. Say *for* and call on volunteers to use the word in context.

Write *for* on the board, and have children spell it as you point to the letters. ***Spell* for *with me,* f-o-r, for.** Then lead children in a chant, clapping on each beat, to help them remember the spelling: *f-o-r, for; f-o-r, for.*

Repeat for the word *have.*

**Word Wall** Have children find the words *for* and *have* on the Word Wall. Remind children to look there when they need to remember how to write the words.

▶ **Practice**

**Reading** Build the following sentences in the pocket chart. Children take turns reading the sentences aloud. Place the pocket chart in the Phonics Center along with additional Picture Cards so that children can practice building and reading sentences.

Display *Higglety Pigglety: A Book of Rhymes,* page 16.

■ Share the rhyme "Baa, Baa, Black Sheep."

■ Reread the first two lines, tracking the print. Have children find and point to the word *have.*

■ Repeat for the remaining lines in the rhyme, having children find the word *for* three times.

Baa, Baa, Black Sheep

Baa, baa, black sheep,
Have you any wool?
Yes, sir, yes, sir,
Three bags full,
One for the master,
One for the dame,
One for the little boy
Who lives in the lane.

a Mother Goose Rhyme

16

*Higglety Pigglety: A Book of Rhymes,* page 16.

Practice Book p. 218

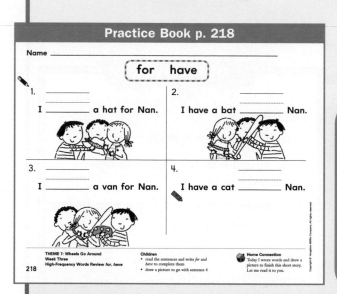

## ▶ Apply

**Practice Book page 218** Children will read and write *for* and *have* as they complete the Practice Book page. On Day 3, they will practice reading *for* and *have* in the **Phonics Library** story "Zig Pig and Dan Cat."

DAY 2

Diagnostic Check

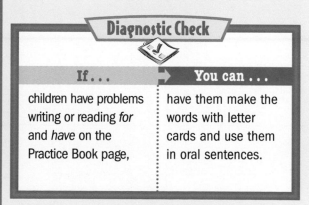

| If... | You can... |
|---|---|
| children have problems writing or reading *for* and *have* on the Practice Book page, | have them make the words with letter cards and use them in oral sentences. |

# Day 2

## OBJECTIVES

**Children**

- read high-frequency words
- create and write sentences with high-frequency words

## MATERIALS

- **Word Cards** *a, and, for, have, I*
- **Picture Cards** *black, green, leaf, sun, white, yellow, zebra*
- **Punctuation Card:** period

# ✓ High-Frequency Word Practice

## ▶ Building Sentences

Tell children that you want to build a sentence about the colors they might use to draw something.

- ■ Display the Word Cards and Picture Cards in random order. Put the Word Card *I* in the pocket chart, and read it.

- ■ *I want the next word to be* have. *Who can find that word? That's right! This word is* have. *Now who can read my sentence so far?*

- ■ Tell children you need a color word next. Have them choose a color word and add the words *for* and *a*.

- ■ Children complete the sentence by choosing an appropriate Picture Card: *I have (yellow) for a _____.*

- ■ Read the sentence together and then continue with new ones: *I have green for a leaf; I have black and white for a zebra.*

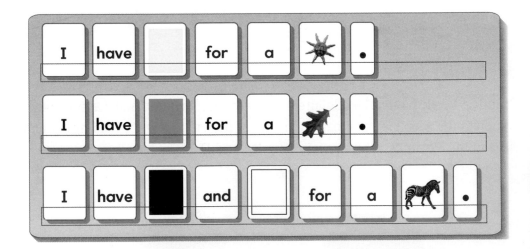

 **Writing Opportunity** Have children copy a sentence from the pocket chart and illustrate it.

# Vocabulary Expansion

## ▶ Words for Travel

Recall *The Wheels on the Bus* with children. Ask: **How did Grandma, Jenny, and Joanna plan to get home?** (by bus) **How did they end up traveling at the end of the story?** (by taxi)

**Listening and Speaking** Write the words *bus* and *taxi* on chart paper and read them. Have children name ways people can travel. List their suggestions on chart paper. Extend the discussion by asking: **How can people travel across the water? How can they travel in the air?**

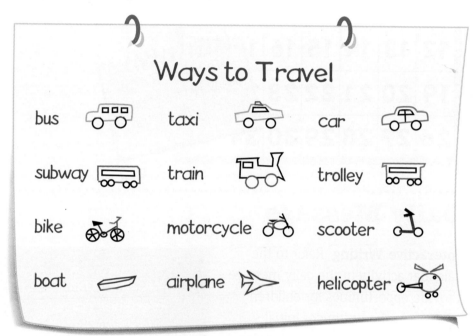

Ways to Travel

bus · taxi · car · subway · train · trolley · bike · motorcycle · scooter · boat · airplane · helicopter

**OBJECTIVES**

**Children**
- brainstorm ways to travel

DAY 2

### At Group Time
## Art Center

On a few sheets of paper, write the stem *I can go for a ride in a ____*. Put the pages in the Art Center. Children can complete the sentence with a drawing of their favorite vehicle.

I can go for a ride in a van.

**English Language Learners**

As you discuss the ways people travel, English language learners can refer to the chart for help in communicating their ideas. Ask questions such as: *Have you been in a taxi? Who has been on a subway? Which is more fun, a boat or an airplane?* Emphasize the difference between prepositions such as *in* and *on*.

## Day at a Glance

### Learning to Read

**Big Book:**

***Vroom, Chugga, Vroom-Vroom***

☑ **Phonics: Blending -ig, Words (dig, zig)** *page T140*

### Word Work

**Building Words,** *page T142*

### Writing & Language

**Shared Writing,** *page T143*

---

  **Half-Day Kindergarten**

☑ Indicates lessons for tested skills. Choose additional activities as time allows.

---

# Opening

## Calendar

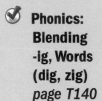

| Sunday | Monday | Tuesday | Wednesday | Thursday | Friday | Saturday |
|--------|--------|---------|-----------|----------|--------|----------|
|  |  |  | 1 | 2 | 3 | 4 |
| 5 | 6 | 7 | 8 | 9 | 10 | 11 |
| 12 | 13 | 14 | 15 | 16 | 17 | 18 |
| 19 | 20 | 21 | 22 | 23 | 24 | 25 |
| 26 | 27 | 28 | 29 | 30 | 31 | |

**Weather Race**

| Sunny | Rainy | Snowy |
|-------|-------|-------|
| ℍℍ I | ℍℍ | ℍℍ |

Call on volunteers to report on the "weather race." How many sunny days have we had so far? How many rainy days? How many more sunny days do we need before sunny days pass rainy days?

## Daily Message

**Interactive Writing** Refer to the calendar activity in the daily message. Provide opportunities for children to share in the writing of initial consonants, high-frequency words, words from known families, and end punctuation.

We are having a
weather race.
Which kind will win?
Let's read about a
race today.

Have children take turns finding Word Wall words with a pointer as you call them out.

## ✓ Daily Phonemic Awareness
### Blending Phonemes

Tell children that you will play an opposites game.

- *I'll say some sounds. You put them together to make a word. Listen: /h/ /ŏ/ /t/. That's right,* hot. *Say the sounds with me: /h/ /ŏ/ /t/,* hot. *Now name an opposite for* hot. (cold)

- Continue the game using the words from the list. Opposites are shown.

### Opposites

| | |
|---|---|
| light (dark) | win (lose) |
| go (stop) | old (young) |
| low (high) | back (front) |
| down (up) | big (little) |

## Getting Ready to Learn

**To help plan their day, tell children that they will**

- listen to the Big Book: *Vroom, Chugga, Vroom-Vroom.*

- read a story called "Zig Pig and Dan Cat."

**Zig Pig and Dan Cat**
by Amy Griffin
illustrated by Amiko Hirao

- explore jobs in the Art Center.

I can put out fires.

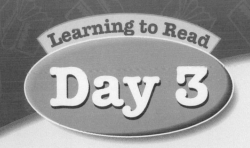

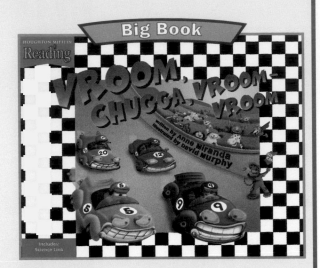

**Big Book**

**Purposes** • concepts of print • story language
• reading strategy • comprehension skill

# Sharing the Big Book
## Oral Language/Comprehension

### ▶ Building Background

Display *Vroom, Chugga, Vroom-Vroom.* Have children share what they remember about the race.

Place a flannel board near the book, and distribute numeral cards for 1–20. Tell children that as their car numbers are named in the beginning of the story, they should put the numbers in a column on the flannel board.

### Strategy: Question

**Student Modeling** Recall with children that asking questions about a story as we read and looking for the answers can make a story more interesting. Take a picture walk through the first few pages of *Vroom, Chugga, Vroom-Vroom.* Ask children what questions they have about a car race that the text and the pictures might answer. Record their questions.

 ### Comprehension Focus: Making Predictions

**Student Modeling** *What predictions could you make about* **Vroom, Chugga, Vroom-Vroom** *from the title and the picture on the cover? Why?* (Clues show it is about a car race: cars' positions, numbers on the cars, fans, the starter, a checked border that looks like the finish-line flag, and a title that sounds like a car engine.)

### ▶ Sharing the Story

Reread the story, pausing for children to put numerals on the flannel board and to discuss these points:

 #### pages 2–3
#### Making Predictions

■ Before reading, say: *Think about car races. What will the drivers do to get ready for the race?* (check the cars; get dressed) Read to confirm predictions.

#### pages 14-17
#### Noting Details

■ Remove flannel numerals as the cars have problems. *Who will help car 7?*

**pages 20–21**

**Concepts of Print: Match spoken words to print; Match words**

■ *Use what you know about letter sounds to find the word* big. *Now find the word* hit. Frame and read *the* on page 20. *Who can match it to the* on *page 21?* Repeat with the word *to.*

 **page 24**

**Making Predictions**

■ *Look at the flannel board. Which car will be the winner?*

**page 30**

**Strategy: Question**

■ Review the questions posed before reading to see if they were answered.

· · · · · · · · · · · · · · · · · · · · · · · · · · · · · · · · · · · · · · · · · · · · ·

▶ **Responding**

Children can take turns playing announcer in a retelling of the story. Each child uses a toy microphone to provide commentary for one or two pages and then passes the microphone to the next announcer.

**Practice Book page 219** Children will complete the page at small group time.

I can put out fires.

I can tell you to go and stop.

**Materials** • drawing paper • crayons or markers

Review the jobs shown in the story: announcer, driver, starter, crew members, firefighters, vendor. Ask children to draw and write about some jobs they would enjoy.

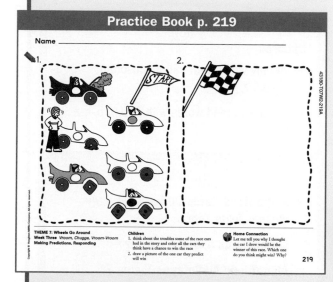

**Practice Book p. 219**

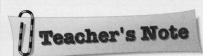

Put *Vroom, Chugga, Vroom-Vroom* in the Math Center with some plastic numerals. Partners can match the numerals to the cars in the story

**DAY 3**

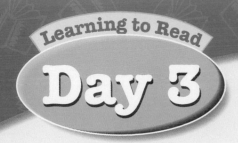

## Learning to Read
# Day 3

# Phonics
## *Blending d -ig, z -ig*

......................................................

▶ **Connect Sounds to Letters**

**Review Consonants *d* and *z*** Play Dudley Duck's song, and have children clap for each /d/ word. Write *D* and *d* on the board, and list words from the song. Repeat with Zelda Zebra and /z/.

**Word Wall**  Point to the word *dig* on the Word Wall. Remind children that they can make words that rhyme with *dig*.

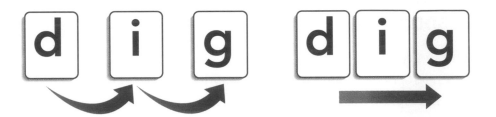

**Blending *-ig* Words** Build the word *dig* letter by letter as you say the sounds. Then take away the *d* and hold up letter card *z*. Put *z* in front of *ig*, and ask children to blend the new word with you: /z/ /ig/, *zig*. Have volunteers blend the sounds and point.

Model blending *-ig* with other familiar consonants to make *big*, *fig*, *pig*, and *rig*. Have children blend as you point.

......................................................

▶ **Apply**

**Practice Book page 220** Children complete the page at small group time.

---

### Practice Book p. 220

Name _____

| big | dig | Zig |

1. _____
   See Dan _____ ? ☺ ☹

2. _____
   See _____ dig? ☺ ☹

3. _____
   Can _____ Zig and Dan fit? ☺ ☹

THEME 7: Wheels Go Around
Week Three
Phonics: d, z, -ig

**Children**
• read the questions and write words ending in -ig to complete them
• mark the smile (yes) or the frown (no) to show whether the picture answers the question

**Home Connection**
Let me read these sentences to you! Then you will help me write the letters Z, i, d, b, and g on separate scraps of paper? Then we can see how many words we can build with them.

220

---

**English Language Learners**

As you work on this lesson, have children say all of the words aloud with you. Check for correct pronunciation of the /ĭ/. You may want to exaggerate the short vowel sound. Also help children recall the meaning of less common words such as *fig* and *rig*.

**T140**  THEME 7: **Wheels Go Around**

**Phonics in Action**

**Phonics Library**

Wheels Go Around

# Applying Phonics Skills and High-Frequency Words

## Phonics/Decoding Strategy

**Teacher-Student Modeling** Discuss using the Strategy to read words in the **Phonics Library** story "Zig Pig and Dan Cat."

### Think Aloud

*The first word in the title begins with capital Z. The sound for Z is /z/. I know the sounds for i, g: /ĭ/, /g/, -ig. Let's blend: /z/ /ig/, Zig. Look at the first picture. We've read about a pig named Zig before, so that name makes sense here.*

Have children read the title silently. Then ask volunteers to model how they blended the words.

Look at the first two pictures together. Make sure children understand that the story takes place at the beach, where there are seashells.

## ▶ Coached Reading

Have children read each page silently before reading with you. Prompts:

**page 16** *Put your finger on the word that tells what Zig and Dan do at the beach.* (dig) Have volunteers model how they blended *dig*.

**page 17** Together, blend *Pig.* Ask: *What other words here rhyme with* Pig? (Zig, dig) *What letters are the same in those rhyming words?* (i, g) *Zig Pig found a shell. What do you think the cat will do?*

**page 18** *Who will read what Dan Cat did when he found a seashell? Read it the way Dan might say it.*

**page 19** *What did Zig and Dan do when they finished digging?* Have volunteers model how they blended *sat.*

---

### Phonics Library

**Purposes**
- apply phonics skills
- apply high-frequency words

**Zig Pig and Dan Cat**
by Amy Griffin
illustrated by Amiko Hirao

15

Zig Pig and Dan Cat
dig for 🐚.

16

Zig Pig can dig.
I have it!

17

Dan Cat can dig.
Here it is!

18

Zig Pig sat.
Dan Cat sat.

19

**DAY 3**

### Home Connection

Children can color the pictures in their take-home version of "Zig Pig and Dan Cat." After rereading on Day 4, they can take it home to read to family members.

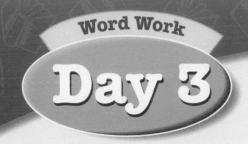
# Day 3

# Building Words

▶ **Word Family: –ig**

Remind children that they know all the sounds and letters to build the word *dig*. Model how to build *dig*, with letter cards. ***Let's stretch out the sounds: /d/ /ĭ/ /g/. How many sounds do you hear? The first sound is /d/. I'll put up a d to spell that. The next sound is /ĭ/. What letter should I choose for that? The last sound is /g/. What letter should I choose for that?***

Blend /d/ /ĭ/ /g/ to read *dig*. Then ask what letter you should change to make the rhyming word *pig*. Remove the *d* and model how to read *pig* by blending /p/ with /ig/.

Continue making and blending -ig words by substituting *b, f, r,* and *z*.

Have small groups work together to build -ig words. Children can use magnetic letters or other manipulative letters in your collection.

# Shared Writing

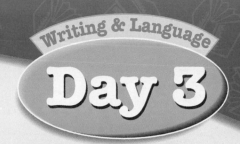

## ▶ Writing a Report

**Speaking and Viewing**  Invite children to help you write a report about some of the things they have learned about wheels during the theme.

Together, make a graphic organizer of ideas to plan what the report will tell. Prompt children by asking questions such as: *How can wheels help us? What kinds of wheels take us where we want to go? What wheels can be fun to use?*

- On the chart, group children's responses into categories of main ideas about wheels.

- Have children brainstorm details to list under each main idea.

- Read through the completed chart with children. Tell them that tomorrow they will help you write a report about wheels, using the ideas on the chart.

**OBJECTIVES**

**Children**
- share ideas for a report on wheels

### Wheels Around Us

| Wheels can help us. | Wheels can be fun. | Wheels help us go places. |
|---|---|---|
| police car | bike | car |
| fire truck | skateboard | brain |
| bus | skates | bus |
| tractor | scooter | subway |
| tow truck | wagon | taxi |

**DAY 3**

# Day 4

## Day at a Glance

### Learning to Read

**Big Books**

*Look for Wheels, Cool Wheels*

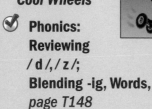

☑ **Phonics:** Reviewing /d/, /z/; Blending -ig, Words, *page T148*

### Word Work

**Building Words,** *page T150*

### Writing & Language

**Interactive Writing,** *page T151*

---

 **Half-Day Kindergarten**

☑ Indicates lessons for tested skills. Choose additional activities as time allows.

---

# Opening

## Calendar

| Sunday | Monday | Tuesday | Wednesday | Thursday | Friday | Saturday |
|--------|--------|---------|-----------|----------|--------|----------|
|        |        |         | 1         | 2        | 3      | 4        |
| 5      | 6      | 7       | 8         | 9        | 10     | 11       |
| 12     | 13     | 14      | 15        | 16       | 17     | 18       |
| 19     | 20     | 21      | 22        | 23       | 24     | 25       |
| 26     | 27     | 28      | 29        | 30       | 31     |          |

When children report the weather, ask if it is a good day for "cool wheels" such as skateboards, skates, or bikes. Have them tell why. Ask how weather might affect the use of other wheels.

## Daily Message

**Interactive Writing** Have children contribute to the daily message by telling how they have learned to use wheels. Call on children to write letters, high-frequency words, and end punctuation.

> Ken can ride a two-wheeled bike.
>
> Amy can roller-skate.
>
> Tanya races little cars.

Remind children that the words on the Word Wall are in ABC order. *I will say the alphabet, and you raise your hand when I come to a letter that begins a word on the wall. A... are there any words that begin with a? Who will point to them and read them?*

# Routines

 ## Daily Phonemic Awareness
### Blending Phonemes

Play "Pat, Pat, Clap" to name different ways in which people travel.

- Slowly pat with children as you say: /b/ /ŭ/ /s/; they clap and say *bus*.

- Continue with other means of transportation.

**Pat, Pat, Clap**

| | |
|---|---|
| cab | bike |
| ship | jet |
| boat | sled |

## Getting Ready to Learn

**To help plan their day, tell children that they will**

- reread the Science Links: *Look for Wheels* and *Cool Wheels*.

- learn to build and read new words.

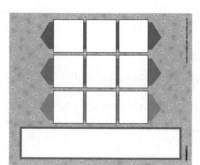

- reread the book called "Zig Pig and Dan Cat."

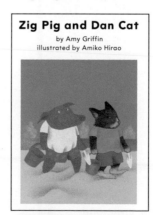

## Learning to Read

# Day 4

**OBJECTIVES**

**Children**

- make predictions
- use the Summarize Strategy
- match spoken words to print
- find matching words

**Big Book**

pages 33–38

**Extra Support**

Before rereading the selections, invite partners to take picture walks through the books. Children can take turns sharing what they remember about the selections, using the pictures as prompts.

# Sharing the Big Books
## *Science Link*

### ▶ Building Background

**Reading for Understanding**  Display *Look for Wheels* and read the title. *Some books tell stories while others give information. Which kind of book is this?* As we read this selection again, look for information about wheels.

 **title page**

### Comprehension Focus: Making Predictions

**Student Modeling**  *Look at the pictures on this title page. What kinds of wheels will we read about?*

### Strategy: Summarize

**Student Modeling** *In an information book, we look for the* main idea, *or what the book is mostly about. What is* Look for Wheels *about? What information can we get from this book?*

 **pages 34-35**
### Concepts of Print: Match spoken words to print; Match words

■ *I will say a word from page 34. You find the word I say. Listen:* for.  Have someone point to the word.  *That's right. Now match the word* for *to the same word on page 35.*

**pages 36–37**

**Compare and Contrast**

■ *How are the wheels on these pages alike? How are they different?*

**page 38**

**Making Judgments**

■ *How would you answer the question on this page?*

### ▶ Responding

**Summarizing** Have partners choose a page of the selection and summarize it for the class, telling what information they got from the words and picture.

## ▶ Building Background

**Rereading for Understanding** Display *Cool Wheels* and read the title. Point out that this selection also gives information about wheels.

**title page**
**Making Judgments**

■ *Look at these wheels. Do you think they are cool? Why?*

**pages 36–37**
**Drawing Conclusions**

■ *What are these men doing?* (competing in races) *How are they different from other bicycle and wheelchair riders you've seen?*

 **page 39**
**Making Predictions**

■ *How do you think these children will use their cool wheels?*

## Responding

**Literature Circle** Have children tell how the selections *Look for Wheels* and *Cool Wheels* are alike. Then have them tell how they are different.

At Group Time
Art Center

> **Materials** • drawing paper • crayons

Have children draw a picture of their favorite kind of wheels and add a label. Some children may be able to find an appropriate word from the selection to copy as a label.

*I like my skates.*

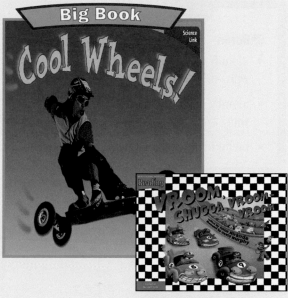
**Big Book**
Science Link
**Cool Wheels!**

VROOM, CHUGGA VROOM

**pages 33–38**

 **OBJECTIVES**

**Children**
• make predictions
• use the Summarize Strategy

**DAY 4**

 **Challenge**
MEETING INDIVIDUAL NEEDS

Some children will be able to use language patterns from *Look for Wheels* or *Cool Wheels* and write a new page to extend the selection. Children can draw or cut out magazine pictures of cool wheels to illustrate their work.

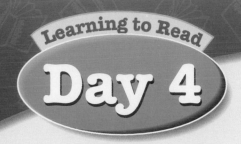
# Phonics

## ✓ Blending -ig Words

▶ **Connect Sounds to Letters**

**Review Consonants d, z** On page 5 of *From Apples to Zebras: A Book of ABCs,* cover the words with self-stick notes. Then display the page. Ask what letter children expect to see first in each word and why. (*d;* begin with /d/) Uncover the words so children can check their answers. Repeat for the z words on page 27.

*From Apples to Zebras: A Book of ABCs*

**Reviewing -ig** Review with children that in order to build a word with *d* or *z* they need a vowel ("helper letter") because every word has a vowel. Ask which Alphafriend stands for the vowel sound /ĭ/. Display Iggy Iguana and have children name other words that start with /ĭ/. (*if, insect, itch*)

Display Letter Cards for *d, i,* and *g. **Watch and listen as I build a word from the Word Wall: /d/ /ĭ/ /g/,** **dig.**

**Blending -ig Words** Put Letter Card f in front of ig. ***Now let's blend my new word: /f/ /ig/,*** **fig.** Continue, having volunteers build and blend *big, pig, rig,* and *zig.*

Tell children they will build more *-ig* words today in the Phonics Center.

## Teacher's Note

During writing, children may ask how to spell words from the *-ig* family. Help children find the word *dig* on the Word Wall and substitute the appropriate initial consonants.

## ▶ Apply

Begin a sentence with the first three words shown and have children read it. For *big*, ask what letter you need to spell each sound. Then have children choose a picture card to complete the sentence.

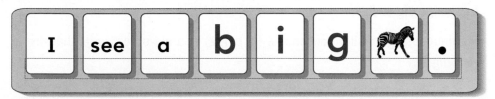

Repeat the activity with *Can a zebra dig?* Then have volunteers read both sentences and blend the *-ig* words.

**Practice Book page 220** Children will complete this page at small group time.

**Phonics Library** In groups today, children will also read *-ig* words as they reread the **Phonics Library** story "Zip Pig and Dan Cat." See suggestion, page T141.

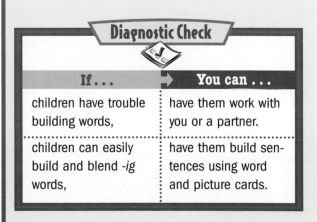

At Group Time

# Phonics Center

Use Phonics Center materials for **Theme 7, Week 3, Day 4**.

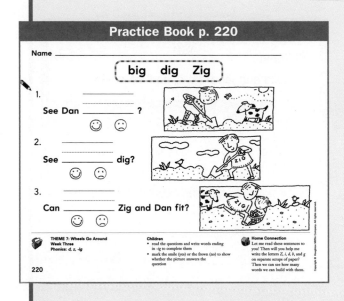

Practice Book p. 220

Name _____

big    dig    Zig

1.
See Dan _____ ?
☺ ☹

2.
See _____ dig?
☺ ☹

3.
Can _____ Zig and Dan fit?
☺ ☹

THEME 7: Wheels Go Around
Week Three
Phonics: d, z, -ig

Children
• read the questions and write words ending in -ig to complete them
• mark the smile (yes) or the frown (no) to show whether the picture answers the question

Home Connection
Let me read these sentences to you! Then will you help me write the letters Z, i, d, b, and g on separate scraps of paper? Then we can see how many words we can build with them.

220

### Diagnostic Check

| If . . . | You can . . . |
|---|---|
| children have trouble building words, | have them work with you or a partner. |
| children can easily build and blend *-ig* words, | have them build sentences using word and picture cards. |

**Phonics** (T149)

DAY 4

## OBJECTIVES

**Children**
- build and read *-ig*, *-it*, and *-at* words

## MATERIALS

- **Letter Cards** *a, b, c, d, f, g, h, i, l, m, p, r, s, t, v, z*

# Building Words

### ▶ Word Families: *-ig*, *-it*, *-at*

Remind children that they have learned to build words by blending sounds together.

- ■ Demonstrate by stretching out the sounds for *dig* as you build *dig* in the pocket chart. Ask a volunteer to find the word *dig* on the Word Wall.

- ■ Remind children that they can build words that rhyme with *dig*. **What should I do to change** dig **to** fig?

- ■ Continue, using familiar consonants (*b, p, r, z*) to build other words that rhyme with *dig*.

Repeat the activity with *-it* words (*lit, bit, fit, pit, sit*) and *-at* words (*bat, fat, hat, mat, pat, rat, sat*).

Have children write some *-ig*, *-it*, or *-at* words on paper. Partners can exchange words and read them.

# Interactive Writing

## ▶ Writing a Report

**Viewing and Speaking** Display the chart from yesterday's shared writing. (See page T143.) Review the chart with children and ask if they would like to add any more ideas. Explain that together you will use the information on it to write a report about wheels.

### Wheels Around Us

| Wheels can help us. | Wheels can be fun. | Whe us. |
|---|---|---|
| police car | bike | ca |
| fire truck | | |

- Choose a category from the chart and explain that the first part of the report will tell about that. Say that the first sentence should tell the reader what the main idea is. Write the heading as a topic sentence. Then have children dictate sentences for each entry listed under that main idea.

- As you write, share the pen with children. Volunteers can supply known consonants, high-frequency words, and words from the -at, -an, -it, and -ig families.

- On another day, add a new paragraph to the report.

## At Group Time
## Writing Center

Invite children to draw pictures to go with the report and to add captions.

This car can help us.

A bike is fun.

**OBJECTIVES**

**Children**
- contribute to a shared report, using ideas from a graphic organizer.

**Portfolio Opportunity**
Save children's drawings and captions for their Portfolios.

DAY 4

# Day 5

## Day at a Glance

### Learning to Read

**Revisiting the Literature:**

*Mr. Gumpy's Motor Car; The Wheels on the Bus; Vroom, Chugga, Vroom-Vroom; Look for Wheels; Cool Wheels; "Zig Pig and Dan Cat"*

 **Phonics Review: Initial Consonants; -at, -an, -it, -ig Words;** *page T156*

### Word Work

**Building Words,** *page T158*

### Writing & Language

**Independent Writing,** *page T159*

---

**✦ Half-Day Kindergarten**

✓ Indicates lessons for tested skills. Choose additional activities as time allows.

---

# Opening

## Calendar

| Sunday | Monday | Tuesday | Wednesday | Thursday | Friday | Saturday |
|---|---|---|---|---|---|---|
| | | | 1 | 2 | 3 | 4 |
| 5 | 6 | 7 | 8 | 9 | 10 | 11 |
| 12 | 13 | 14 | 15 | 16 | 17 | 18 |
| 19 | 20 | 21 | 22 | 23 | 24 | 25 |
| 26 | 27 | 28 | 29 | 30 | 31 | |

rainy
bus
first
last

Review with children any words that were posted next to the calendar this week. Call on volunteers to use the words in oral sentences.

## Daily Message

**Modeled Writing** After writing the message, allow each child to circle a letter they can name or box a word they can read. Children will enjoy seeing how much of the message they "know."

> Today is Friday.
> It is Kim's turn to
> water the plants
> for the week-end.

## Word Wall

Distribute cards for words on the Word Wall. Have volunteers take turns using a pointer and reading a word on the wall. The child with the matching word card stands and reads the card.

# Routines

## Daily Phonemic Awareness
### Blending Phonemes

- Read Aloud "Stop and Go" on page 30 of *Higglety Pigglety.*

- Say *I'll say some sounds. You put them together to make a word from the poem. Listen:* /m/ /ē/ /n/ /z/ ... *That's right,* means. *Say the sounds with me:* /m/ /ē/ /n/ /z/, means.

- Continue with other one-syllable words from the poem. Choose words with two or three sounds.

*Higglety Pigglety: A Book of Rhymes,* page 30

# Getting Ready to Learn

To help plan their day, tell children that they will

- talk about books they've read in *Wheels Go Around.*

- take home a story they can read.

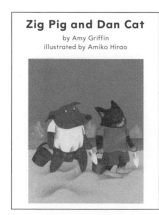

- write about favorite wheels in their journals.

**DAY 5**

# Revisiting the Literature

▶ **Literature Discussion**

Display the books you have shared this week. Use these suggestions to help children recall the selections:

■ Ask what happened when *Mr. Gumpy's Motor Car* was caught in the rain.

■ Have children explain the problem Grandma and the girls had in *The Wheels on the Bus.*

■ Page through *Vroom, Chugga, Vroom-Vroom.* Have children tell their favorite part of the story and why.

■ Take a picture walk and call on volunteers to summarize *Look for Wheels* and *Cool Wheels.* Ask children about other special wheels they have seen.

■ Have children vote for their favorite book. Read aloud the text of the winner.

**Comprehension: Making Predictions** Remind children that good readers make predictions about what a book is about and what will happen next in it. Display the cover or title page of each book. *Which title and book cover do you think tells best what the book is about? Why?*

## www.eduplace.com
Log on to **Education Place** for more activities relating to Wheels Go Round.

## www.bookadventure.org
This Internet reading-incentive program provides thousands of titles for children to read.

# Dig, Zig Pig!
## On My Way Practice Reader

MEETING INDIVIDUAL NEEDS

On My Way
Practice Readers

### ▶ Preparing to Read

**Building Background**  Tell children that this story is about a character they have met before. Have them read his name. (Zig Pig) Then explain that Zig Pig drives a *rig,* which means equipment for a special job. Ask what this rig is used for. (digging)

### ▶ Guiding the Reading

Walk through the story, discussing the pictures. Use the ideas below to prepare children for reading on their own.

**page 2:**  *Zig Pig hopes to find something while he digs. What does the word something start with? Can you find that word on this page? What does Zig Pig think he might find?*

**page 3:**  *Zig Pig hears a noise. What happened?* (The rig hit something.)

**page 4:**  *What did Zig Pig find this time? How does he feel about that?*

**pages 6–7:**  *Has Zig Pig quit digging yet? When you read this part, you will see that he does not want to quit! Find the word not on page 6. What do you think Zig Pig will find?*

**Prompting Strategies**  Listen and observe children as they "whisper read." Use prompts such as these to help them apply strategies:

- *Try again. This page names what Zig Pig found.*

- *You said _____. Does that have the right sounds? Does it make sense?*

- *You were almost right. Read the line again and see if you can find the problem.*

### ▶ Responding

Have children take turns reading aloud their favorite parts. Then ask them to draw what *they* would like to find in a treasure chest.

### Leveled Books

The materials listed below provide reading practice for children at different levels.

#### Little Big Books

#### Little Readers for Guided Reading

#### Houghton Mifflin Classroom Bookshelf

DAY 5

**Home Connection**

Remind children to share the **take-home** version of "Dig, Zig Pig!" with their families.

# Phonics Review
## ✓ Consonants, Word Families

### ▶ Review

**OBJECTIVES**

**Children**

- build and read words with initial consonants and short *a* + *t*, short *a* + *n*, short *i* + *t*, short *i* + *g*

- make sentences with high-frequency words

**MATERIALS**

- **Word Cards** *a, and, for, go, have, her, I, is, like, my, see, to*

- **Picture Cards** for sentence building

- **Punctuation Cards:** period, question mark

Tell children that today they will take turns being word builders and word readers. Have a group of word builders stand with you at the chalkboard.

- *Let's build* dig. *First, count the sounds. I know* d *stands for* /d/. *I also know that* i *stands for* /ĭ/ *and* g *stands for* /g/. *Let's write these letters.*

- Have children copy *dig* on the board and blend the sounds.

- Now erase the *d* and add *f* in front of your letters. Children copy and ask the rest of the class (word readers) what new word they've made.

- Ask a new group to change places with the first one. At your direction, they erase the *f*, write *p*, and ask the word readers to say the new word.

- Continue until everyone builds a word by replacing one letter. Examples: *rig, zig, big; bit, pit, quit, sit; sat, pat, cat, hat, vat; van, tan, fan, man.*

# High-Frequency Word Review

✓ *I, see, my, like, a, to, and, go, is, here, for, have*

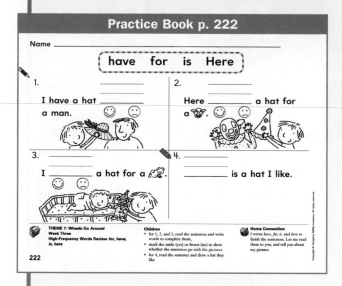

## ▶ Review

Give each small group the Word Cards, Picture Cards, and Punctuation Card needed to make a sentence. Each child holds one card. Children stand and arrange themselves to make a sentence for others to read; as a clue, remind them that a sentence starts with a capital letter.

Repeat with other sentences.

## ▶ Apply

**Practice Book page 222** Children can complete this page independently and read it to you during small group time.

**Phonics Library** Have children take turns reading aloud to the class. Each child might read one page of "Zig Pig and Dan Cat" or a favorite **Phonics Library** selection from the previous theme. Remind readers to share the pictures!

Questions for discussion:

- *Do you hear any rhyming words in either story? What letters are the same in those words?*

- *Find a word that starts with the same sound as Dudley Duck's name. What is the letter? What is the sound? Find a word that starts like Zelda Zebra's name.*

- *This week we practiced reading the words* for *and* have *on the Word Wall. Find the words* for *and* have *in "Zig Pig and Dan Cat."*

### 📎 Teacher's Note

You will need to make word cards for *Can* and *big* to build the sample sentences. You may wish to incorporate additional *-an* and *-ig* words in the Review.

### 🗃 Portfolio Opportunity

Save the Practice Book page to show children's recognition of high-frequency words

### Diagnostic Check

| If... | You can... |
|---|---|
| children need help remembering the consonant sounds, | have them match **Alphafriend Cards** to letter cards. |
| children pause at high-frequency words in **Phonics Library** selections, | have partners practice reading the words on the Word Wall. |

**DAY 5**

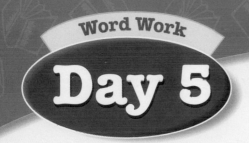
# Day 5

## OBJECTIVES

**Children**

- build and read *-an, -it, -ig* words

## MATERIALS

- **Letter Cards** *a, b, c, D, f, g, h, i, l, m, N, p, r, s, t, v, z*

# Building Words

▶ **Word Families**

Model how to build *an*, stretching out the sounds. Along the bottom of the pocket chart, place the letters *b, c, D, f, m, N, p, r, t,* and *v*. **Let's build the word can. What letter should I take from here to make can?** Have a volunteer take the letter *c* and place it in front of *an*.

Continue building *-at* words, using initial consonants *f, m, N, p, r, t,* and *v*. On chart paper, keep a list of all the *-an* words you make, and reread the list together. Examples: *an, can, fan, man, Nan, pan, ran, tan, van.*

Continue the activity with *-it* and *-ig* words. Examples: *it, bit, fit, hit, lit, pit, sit; dig, big, fig, pig, rig, zig.*

Have small groups work together to build *-an, -it,* and *-ig* words with alphabet blocks or other materials. Children can check the Word Bank sections of their journals to see if there are additional words they would like to add.

# Independent Writing

**Journals** Explain that today children will write sentences to tell about their favorite kind of wheels.

- Pass out the journals.

- *This week we talked about the different ways people can travel, including ways to travel on the water and in the air. What new words could you put in your journal?*

- *We also worked together to write a report on wheels. Let's look at our charts. We had three main ideas and lots of details. Which main idea might you like to write about?*

- Have children draw and write about their favorite kind of wheels. Remind them that they can refer to classroom charts, the Word Wall, and the theme books as they write.

- If time permits, invite children to share what they've written with the class.

I go fast.

My wagon helps me.

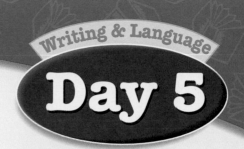

## OBJECTIVES

**Children**
- write independently

## MATERIALS

- journals

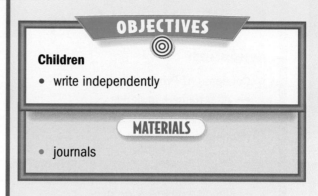

**Portfolio Opportunity**

Mark journal entries you would like to share with parents. Allow children to choose their best efforts or favorite works for sharing as well.

DAY 5

# Theme Assessment Wrap-Up

## Emerging Literacy Survey

**Areas Assessed:**

**1.** **Concepts of Print**
- Letter name knowledge
- Sound-letter association

**2.** **Phonemic Awareness**
- Rhyme
- Beginning sounds
- Blending onsets and rimes
- Segmenting onsets and rimes
- Blending phonemes
- Segmenting phonemes

**3.** **Beginning Reading and Writing**
- Word recognition
- Word writing
- Sentence dictation
- Oral reading

## ▶ Monitoring Literacy Development

If you have administered the **Emerging Literacy Survey** as a baseline assessment of the skills children brought with them to Kindergarten, this might be a good time to re-administer all or part of it to chart progress, to identify areas of strength and need, and to test the need for early intervention.

Use the **Observation Checklist** throughout the theme to write notes indicating whether each child has a beginning, developing, or proficient understanding of reading, writing, and language concepts. (See facing page.)

## ▶ Assessing Student Progress

**Formal Assessment** The **Integrated Theme Test** and the **Theme Skills Test** are formal assessments used to evaluate children's performance on theme objectives.

- The **Integrated Theme Test** assesses children's progress as readers and writers in a format that reflects instruction. Simple decodable texts test reading skills in context.

- The **Theme Skills Test** assesses children's mastery of specific reading and language arts skills taught in the theme.

# Observation Checklist

Name _____     Date _____

| | Beginning | Developing | Proficient |
|---|---|---|---|
| **Listening Comprehension**<br>• Participates in shared and choral reading | | | |
| • Listens to story attentively | | | |
| **Phonemic Awareness**<br>• Blends phonemes | | | |
| • Identifies beginning sound | | | |
| **Phonics**<br>• Recognizes sounds for initial consonants *d* and *z* | | | |
| • Builds words with word family *-ig* | | | |
| **Concepts of Print**<br>• Uses a capital at the beginning of a sentence | | | |
| • Uses end punctuation (period, question mark) | | | |
| **Reading**<br>• Reads simple decodable texts | | | |
| • Reads the high-frequency words *for, have* | | | |
| **Comprehension**<br>• Recognizes text organization; can summarize | | | |
| • Understands cause and effect | | | |
| • Can make inferences, predictions | | | |
| **Writing and Language**<br>• Writes simple phrases | | | |
| • Participates in shared and interactive writing | | | |

For each child, write notes or checkmarks in the appropriate columns.

# Theme Resources

## Resources for *Wheels Go Around*

## Contents

# My Bonnie Lies Over the Ocean

*Traditional*

*Moderately*

**Use this music for Dudley Duck's song.**

# Li'l Liza Jane

Use this music for Zelda Zebra's song.

# The Wheels on the Bus

# Word List

In Themes 1 through 3, the Phonics Library stories are wordless.

## Theme 1

▶ **Phonics Skills:** none taught in this theme
▶ **High-Frequency Words:** none taught in this theme

**Phonics Library, Week 1:**
*We Go to School*
  wordless story

**Phonics Library, Week 2:**
*See What We Can Do*
  wordless story

**Phonics Library, Week 3:**
*We Can Make It*
  wordless story

## Theme 2

▶ **Phonics Skills:** Initial consonants s, m, r
▶ **High-Frequency Words:** I, see

**Phonics Library, Week 1:**
*My Red Boat*
  wordless story

**Phonics Library, Week 2:**
*Look at Me*
  wordless story

**Phonics Library, Week 3:**
*The Parade*
  wordless story

## Theme 3

▶ **Phonics Skills:** Initial consonants t, b, n
▶ **High-Frequency Words:** my, like

**Phonics Library, Week 1:**
*The Birthday Party*
  wordless story

**Phonics Library, Week 2:**
*Baby Bear's Family*
  wordless story

**Phonics Library, Week 3:**
*Cat's Surprise*
  wordless story

## Theme 4

▶ **Phonics Skills:** Initial consonants h, v, c; words with -at
▶ **High-Frequency Words:** a, to

**Phonics Library, Week 1:**
*Nat at Bat*
  Words with -at: at, bat, hat, Nat, sat
  High-Frequency Words: my, see

**Phonics Library, Week 2:**
*A Vat*
  Words with -at: hat, mat, rat, vat
  High-Frequency Word: a

**Phonics Library, Week 3:**
*Cat Sat*
  Words with -at: bat, cat, hat, mat, sat
  High-Frequency Words: my, see

## Theme 5

▶ **Phonics Skills:** Initial consonants p, g, f; words with -an
▶ **High-Frequency Words:** and, go

**Phonics Library, Week 1:**
*Nat, Pat, and Nan*
  Words with -an: Nan, ran
  Words with -at: Nat, Pat, sat
  High-Frequency Words: and, see

**Phonics Library, Week 2:**
*Go, Cat!*
  Words with -an: Nan, ran, Van
  Words with -at: Cat, Pat, sat
  High-Frequency Word: go

**Phonics Library, Week 3:**
*Pat and Nan*
  Words with -an: fan, Nan, ran
  Words with -at: Pat, sat
  High-Frequency Words: a, and, go

## Theme 6

▶ **Phonics Skills:** Initial consonants l, k, qu; words with -it
▶ **High-Frequency Words:** is, here

**Phonics Library, Week 1:**
*Can It Fit?*
  Words with -it: fit, it, sit
  Words with -an: can, man, van
  High-Frequency Words: a, go, I, is, my

**Phonics Library, Week 2:**
*Kit*
  Words with -it: bit, fit, it, Kit, lit, sit
  Words with -an: can, pan
  Words with -at: hat
  High-Frequency Words: a, here, I

**Phonics Library, Week 3:**
*Fan*
  Words with -it: bit, quit
  Words with -an: an, Fan
  Words with -at: sat
  High-Frequency Words: a, here, is

## Theme 7

▶ **Phonics Skills:** Initial consonants d, z; words with -ig
▶ **High-Frequency Words:** for, have

**Phonics Library, Week 1:**
*Big Rig*
  Words with -ig: Big, dig, Rig
  Words with -it: pit
  Words with -an: can, Dan
  High-Frequency Words: a, for

**Phonics Library, Week 2:**
*Tan Van*
  Words with -ig: Pig, Zig
  Words with -it: it
  Words with -an: can, Dan, ran, tan, van
  Words with -at: Cat, sat
  High-Frequency Words: a, have, I, is

**Phonics Library, Week 3:**
*Zig Pig and Dan Cat*
  Words with -ig: dig, Pig, Zig
  Words with -it: it
  Words with -an: can, Dan
  Words with -at: Cat, sat
  High-Frequency Words: and, for, have, here, I, is

## Theme 8

▶ **Phonics Skills:** Consonant x; words with -ot, -ox
▶ **High-Frequency Words:** said, the

**Phonics Library, Week 1:**
*Dot Got a Big Pot*
**Words with** -ot: Dot, got, hot, lot, pot
**Words with** -ig: big
**Words with** -it: it
**Words with** -an: Nan
**Words with** -at: Nat, sat
**High-Frequency Words:** a, and, I, is, like, said

**Phonics Library, Week 2:**
*The Big, Big Box*
**Words with** -ox: box, Fox
**Words with** -ot: not
**Words with** -ig: big
**Words with** -it: bit, fit, hit, it
**Words with** -an: can, Dan, Fan
**Words with** -at: Cat, hat, mat, sat
**High-Frequency Words:** a, is, my, said, the

**Phonics Library, Week 3:**
*A Pot for Dan Cat*
**Words with** -ot: pot
**Words with** -ox: Fox
**Words with** -ig: big
**Words with** -it: fit
**Words with** -an: can, Dan, Fan, ran
**Words with** -at: Cat, sat
**High-Frequency Words:** a, and, see, said

## Theme 9

▶ **Phonics Skills:** Initial consonants w, y; words with -et, -en
▶ **High-Frequency Words:** play, she

**Phonics Library, Week 1:**
*Get Set! Play!*
**Words with** -et: get, set, wet, yet
**Words with** -ot: got, not
**Words with** -ox: Fox
**Words with** -ig: Pig
**Words with** -an: can
**High-Frequency Words:** a, play, said

**Phonics Library, Week 2:**
*Ben*
**Words with** -en: Ben, Hen, men, ten
**Words with** -et: get, net, pet, vet, yet
**Words with** -ot: got, not
**Words with** -ox: box, Fox
**Words with** -it: it
**Words with** -an: can
**High-Frequency Words:** a, I, my, play, said, she, the

**Phonics Library, Week 3:**
*Pig Can Get Wet*
**Words with** -et: get, wet
**Words with** -ot: got, not
**Words with** -ig: big, Pig, wig
**Words with** -it: sit
**Words with** -an: can
**Words with** -at: Cat, sat
**High-Frequency Words:** a, my, play, said, she

## Theme 10

▶ **Phonics Skills:** Initial consonant j; words with -ug, -ut
▶ **High-Frequency Words:** are, he

**Phonics Library, Week 1:**
*Ken and Jen*
**Words with** -ug: dug
**Words with** -en: Ken, Jen
**Words with** -et: wet
**Words with** -ot: hot
**Words with** -ig: big, dig
**Words with** -it: it, pit
**High-Frequency Words:** a, and, are, is

**Phonics Library, Week 2:**
*It Can Fit*
**Words with** -ut: but, nut
**Words with** -ug: jug, lug, rug
**Words with** -ox: box
**Words with** -ot: not
**Words with** -ig: big
**Words with** -it: fit, it
**Words with** -an: can, tan, van
**Words with** -at: fat, hat
**High-Frequency Words:** a, he, see, she

**Phonics Library, Week 3:**
*The Bug Hut*
**Words with** -ut: but
**Words with** -ug: Bug, hug, lug
**Words with** -ox: box
**Words with** -ot: Dot, got, not
**Words with** -ig: Big, jig
**Words with** -an: can, Jan
**Words with** -at: fat, hat
**High-Frequency Words:** a, here, is, she, the

# Cumulative Word List

By the end of Theme 10, children will have been taught the skills necessary to read the following words.

**Words with -at**
at, bat, cat, fat, hat, mat, Nat, Pat, rat, sat, vat

**Words with -an**
an, ban, can, Dan, fan, Jan, man, Nan, pan, ran, tan, van

**Words with -it**
bit, fit, hit, it, kit, lit, pit, quit, sit, wit

**Words with -ig**
big, dig, fig, jig, pig, rig, wig, zig

**Words with -ot**
cot, dot, got, hot, jot, lot, not, pot, rot, tot

**Words with -ox**
box, fox, ox

**Words with -et**
bet, get, jet, let, met, net, pet, set, vet, wet, yet

**Words with -en**
Ben, den, hen, Jen, Ken, men, pen, ten

**Words with -ug**
bug, dug, hug, jug, lug, mug, rug, tug

**Words with -ut**
but, cut, hut, jut, nut, rut

**High-Frequency Words**
a, and, are, for, go, have, he, here, I, is, like, my, play, said, see, she, the, to

# Technology Resources

**American Melody**
P. O. Box 270
Guilford, CT  06473
800-220-5557

**Audio Bookshelf**
174 Prescott Hill Road
Northport, ME  04849
800-234-1713

**Baker & Taylor**
100 Business Court Drive
Pittsburgh, PA  15205
800-775-2600

**BDD Audio**
1540 Broadway
New York, NY  10036
800-223-6834

**Big Kids Productions**
1606 Dywer Avenue
Austin, TX  78704
800-477-7811
www.bigkidsvideo.com

**Blackboard Entertainment**
2647 International
Boulevard
Suite 853
Oakland, CA  94601
800-968-2261
www.blackboardkids.com

**Books on Tape**
P. O. Box 7900
Newport Beach, CA  92658
800-626-3333

**Filmic Archives**
The Cinema Center
Botsford, CT  06404
800-366-1920
www.filmicarchives.com

**Great White Dog Picture Company**
10 Toon Lane
Lee, NH  03824
800-397-7641
www.greatwhitedog.com

**HarperAudio**
10 E. 53rd Street
New York, NY  10022
800-242-7737

**Houghton Mifflin Company**
222 Berkeley Street
Boston, MA  02116
800-225-3362

**Informed Democracy**
P. O. Box 67
Santa Cruz, CA  95063
831-426-3921

**JEF Films**
143 Hickory Hill Circle
Osterville, MA  02655
508-428-7198

**Kimbo Educational**
P. O. Box 477
Long Branch, NJ  07740
900-631-2187

**The Learning Company (dist. for Broderbund)**
1 Athenaeum Street
Cambridge, MA  02142
800-716-8506
www.learningco.com

**Library Video Co.**
P. O. Box 580
Wynnewood, PA  19096
800-843-3620

**Listening Library**
One Park Avenue
Old Greenwich, CT  06870
800-243-45047

**Live Oak Media**
P. O. Box 652
Pine Plains, NY  12567
800-788-1121
liveoak@taconic.net

**Media Basics**
Lighthouse Square
P. O. Box 449
Guilford, CT  06437
800-542-2505
www.mediabasicsvideo.com

**Microsoft Corp.**
One Microsoft Way
Redmond, WA  98052
800-426-9400
www.microsoft.com

**National Geographic Society**
1145 17th Street N. W.
Washington, D. C.  20036
800-368-2728
www.nationalgeographic.com

**New Kid Home Video**
1364 Palisades Beach Road
Santa Monica, CA  90401
310-451-5164

**Puffin Books**
345 Hudson Street
New York, NY  10014
212-366-2000

**Rainbow Educational Media**
4540 Preslyn Drive
Raleigh, NC  27616
800-331-4047

**Random House Home Video**
201 E. 50th Street
New York, NY  10022
212-940-7620

**Recorded Books**
270 Skipjack Road
Prince Frederick, MD  20678
800-638-1304
www.recordedbooks.com

**Sony Wonder**
Dist. by Professional
Media Service
19122 S. Vermont Avenue
Gardena, CA  90248
800-223-7672

**Spoken Arts**
8 Lawn Avenue
P. O. Box 100
New Rochelle, NY  10802
800-326-4090

**SRA Media**
220 E. Danieldale Road
DeSoto, TX  75115
800-843-8855

**Sunburst Communications**
101 Castleton Street
P. O. Box 100
Pleasantville, NY  10570
800-321-7511
www.sunburst.com

**SVE & Churchill Media**
6677 North Northwest
Highway
Chicago, IL  60631
800-829-1900

**Tom Snyder Productions**
80 Coolidge Hill Road
Watertown, MA  02472
800-342-0236
www.tomsnyder.com

**Troll Communications**
100 Corporate Drive
Mahwah, NJ  07430
800-526-5289

**Weston Woods**
12 Oakwood Avenue
Norwalk, CT  06850-1318
800-243-5020
www.scholastic.com

# Index

*Boldface* page references indicate formal strategy and skill instruction.

## N

**Newsletters.** *See* Home connection.

## O

**Oral composition.** *See* Speaking activities.

**Oral language development,** *T15, T18–T19, T32, T40, T62–T65, T69, T72–T73, T82, T96, T118–T121, T125, T128–T129, T138–T139*
 *See also* Listening; Speaking activities.

**Oral reading.** *See* Reading modes; Rereading.

**Oral Reading Fluency.** *See* Fluency, reading.

**Oral summary.** *See* Summarizing.

## P

**Parent involvement.** *See* Home connection.

**Performance assessment.** *See* Assessment.

**Personal response.** *See* Responding to literature.

**Phonemic awareness**
 beginning sounds, **T20, T66–T67, T74–T75, T122–T123**
 blending phonemes, **T17, T27, T34, T39, T47, T61, T71, T81, T95, T98–T99, T103, T117, T127, T137, T140, T145, T148–T149, T153**

**Phonics,** *T13, T21, T43, T67, T75, T99, T123, T131, T149*
 blending, **T17, T27, T34, T39, T42–T443, T47, T61, T71, T81, T90, T95, T98–T99, T103, T117, T127, T137, T140, T145, T148–T149, T153**

consonants, initial
 *d, T12, T20–T21, T26, T42, T123, T130–T131, T140, T156*
 *l, T67, T74*
 *p, T67, T74*
 *r, T130*
 *z, T67, T74–T75, T90, T123, T130–T131, T140*
 word families, **T36, T44, T52, T92, T100, T106, T108, T142, T150, T156, T158**

**Phonics Library titles**
 "Big Rig," *T35, T43, T107*
 "Tan Van," *T91, T99, T105, T107*
 "Zig Pig and Dan Cat," *T133, T141, T149, T157*

**Phonological awareness.** *See* Phonemic awareness.

**Predicting outcomes.** *See* Comprehension skills.

**Predictions, making and checking**
 while reading, *T118*

**Print awareness.** *See* Concepts of print.

**Prior knowledge.** *See* Background, building.

## R

**Reading fluency.** *See* Fluency.

**Reading log.** *See* Journal.

**Reading modes**
 oral reading, *T49, T105*
 teacher read aloud, *iv, T10–T11, T62–T65, T118–T121*
 *See also* Rereading.

**Reading strategies.** *See* Strategies, reading.

**Reads on and rereads.** *See* Strategies, reading.

**Rereading**
 for comprehension, *T147*
 orally, *T49, T105*

**Responding to literature, options for**
 discussion, *T48, T104, T129, T154*
 personal response, *T19, T73*

**Retelling**
 story, *T33, T88, T139*

**Routines**
 daily, *T4–T5, T56–T57, T112–T113*
 opening, *T8–T9, T16–T17, T38–T39, T46–T47, T60–T61, T70–T71, T80–T81, T94–T95, T102–T103, T116–T117, T126–T127, T136–T137, T144–T145, T152–T153*

## S

**Science activities.** *See* Cross-curricular links.

**Sentence building,** *T22, T24, T51, T68, T76, T78, T107, T124, T132, T134, T149*

**Sequence of events, noting.** *See* Comprehension skills.

**Shared writing,** **T37, T93, T143**

**Sight words.** *See* High-frequency words.

**Skills links**
 science, *iv, T96–T97, T146–T147*

**Sounding out words.** *See* Phonemic awareness, blending.

**Sound-spelling patterns.** *See* Phonics.

**Speaking activities**
 literature discussion (*See* Responding to literature.)
 retelling (*See* Retelling.)
 summary (*See* Summarizing, oral summaries.)
 weather reports, *T16, T136*
 *See also* Reading modes; Rereading.

**Storytelling.** *See* Retelling.

**Strategic reading.** *See* Strategies, reading.